THE TRANSFORMATION
OF STRATEGIC AFFAIRS

LAWRENCE FREEDMAN

ADELPHI PAPER 379

The International Institute for Strategic Studies

Arundel House | 13–15 Arundel Street | Temple Place | London | WC2R 3DX | UK

ADELPHI PAPER 379

First published March 2006 by **Routledge**
4 Park Square, Milton Park, Abingdon, Oxon, OX14 4RN

for **The International Institute for Strategic Studies**
Arundel House, 13–15 Arundel Street, Temple Place, London, WC2R 3DX, UK
www.iiss.org

Simultaneously published in the USA and Canada by **Routledge**
270 Madison Ave., New York, NY 10016

Routledge is an imprint of Taylor & Francis, an Informa Business

© 2006 The International Institute for Strategic Studies

DIRECTOR John Chipman
EDITOR Tim Huxley
MANAGER FOR EDITORIAL SERVICES Ayse Abdullah
ASSISTANT EDITOR Jessica Delaney
PRODUCTION Jesse Simon
COVER IMAGE Getty Images
SMALLER IMAGES Courtesy US Army, US Air Force and Department of Defense

Printed and bound in Great Britain by Bell & Bain Ltd, Thornliebank, Glasgow

British Library Cataloguing in Publication Data
A catalogue record for this book is available from the British Library

Library of Congress Cataloguing in Publication Data

ISBN 0-415-40724-9
ISSN 0567-932X

Contents

INTRODUCTION

A recurrent theme in much contemporary writing on strategy is that war in its classical form, involving set-piece battles between regular armies, does not have much of a future.[1] This issue is particularly important for the United States. Its international role relies on an ability to take on all comers in all circumstances. It has superior capabilities for nuclear exchanges and conventional battle, but capabilities at the level upon which most contemporary conflict takes place have been found wanting when recently put to the test. After Vietnam, the US armed forces demonstrated a marked aversion to counter-insurgency operations and dismissed peacekeeping as an inappropriate use of capabilities geared to high-intensity combat. They acknowledged a lack of comparative advantage in low-intensity operations, as they prepared for bigger things, but they also took comfort in the apparent lack of any strategic imperative that would oblige them to engage in distant civil wars. On occasion, as in Somalia, the US government chose to engage, but the military leadership left little doubt that as far as it was concerned this was a bad choice, and, at least in this case, experience seemed to prove it right. Afghanistan and Iraq, however, have created new strategic imperatives and so engagement has become unavoidable, continuous and vexatious. The US would not be the first apparently unbeatable military power to find itself undone by an inability to take seriously or even to comprehend enemies that rely on their ability to emerge out of the shadows of civil society, preferring minor skirmish to major battle, accepting no possibility for decisive victory but instead aiming to unsettle, harass, demoralise, humiliate and eventually to wear down their opponents. This was, after all, the basis of many successful 'wars of national liberation' against colonial powers. Meanwhile, the strategic imperatives that would justify the large-scale investments in nuclear and conventional capabilities that dominate the Pentagon's budget are no longer self-evident.

This paper does not argue that major regular wars will not occur in the future or that it is pointless to prepare for them. There have been many predictions of the obsolescence of major war that turned out almost immediately to be wrong.[2] These predictions were often quite correct on the irrationality of warfare but wrong on their assumptions that rationality would prevail, or at least in terms of appreciating the short-term conditions that might lead countries to act so decisively against their long-term interests. While the impulse to acquire colonies or to secure markets through conquest may never again reach nineteenth-century proportions, different impulses towards inter-state war may arise, perhaps as a result of conflicts over scarce resources or in the wake of great environmental upheavals. Perhaps the current consensus on the irrationality of major war depends more than is appreciated on a calculation of the prevailing balance of power; if guards should be lowered or offensive capabilities suddenly increased, then these calculations may start to look quite different. Given these possibilities, some expenditure on nuclear and conventional forces might be prudent to deter great power confrontations (although this sort of claim is impossible to prove). The capacity for regular war is not confined to the major powers and it would not be surprising if one of the many territorial disputes among minor powers reached such a critical point that resort to arms seemed to be the only way to achieve a resolution. These uncertainties mean that it is highly likely that governments will continue to make provisions for regular war and to train their armed forces accordingly. Even while they may accept that a full-blown capacity for regular war may never be used, there are aspects of contemporary conflict which still involve high-intensity operations and can take advantage of the most advanced weapons systems.

Nor is it necessarily the case that the recent pattern of Western engagement in irregular warfare will continue, even though they now have experiences at home in an extreme, if only sporadic, form. In the conflicts that now demand immediate attention it is suicide bombers who appear to be most threatening. As agents of terror they might turn up almost anywhere, including in city centres, with a strategic purpose that appears little more than an expression of a generalised sense of global grievance; alternatively they act as the shock troops of more localised but intensely vicious insurgencies. If this represents a trend in how to express personality disorders then it may last for some time. If it is, however, strategic in inspiration then it may prosper or fizzle out depending on whether it is setting back or advancing the causes that it is supposed to serve.[3]

There is an argument that the risks of having to cope with acts of indiscriminate ferocity could be reduced if states were to refrain from future engagement with the more troubled parts of the world. During the 1990s it seemed reasonable to suppose that Western countries would have to engage in distant conflicts – even when their interests were at most indirectly involved – to protect vulnerable populations at risk from internal repression or inter-communal disorder. During the present decade it has become evident that Western interests could be more directly at stake but also that they are not so easy to secure through the use of force. It is quite possible that in response to events in Iraq there will be an attempt to wind down existing Western commitments and a reluctance to take on more. If the real need is to prevent terrorist acts within Western countries then that may depend more on the quality of work by intelligence agencies and the police than the use of armed forces in expeditionary roles.

Nonetheless, this paper assumes that, for the moment, the most perplexing problems of security policy surround irregular rather than regular war. It is, of course, a matter of enormous relief that these wars lack the sense of ultimate, existential danger posed by the major wars of the past, but that is also the reason why they are so perplexing. When the security of the state is threatened by a large and self-evidently hostile enemy then all social and economic resources can be mobilised in response. When, by contrast, there is a debate to be had about the nature of the threat and whether matters are made better or worse by direct action, military operations appear to be more discretionary and national mobilisation on even a modest scale becomes more difficult. Describing and quantifying the risks becomes harder, complicating the terrible calculus of costs and benefits that policy-makers face when embarking on any military operation, whereby collections of lives are weighed against one another, or the tangibles of human and physical destruction are set against the intangibles of high principle and even reputation. Even when military action is chosen, operations undertaken in politically complex settings can be full of surprises and lead to new missions and new rationales. The surprises often result from a failure to understand the strategic cultures and agendas of both friends and enemies, and the mixtures of motives and attitudes that influence their behaviour. Coping with these new conditions presents a substantial challenge to strategists.

The experience of Iraq since 2003 can and will be taken to reinforce the principled and prudential reasons to challenge the very idea that war might be used as a means of achieving supposedly liberal goals. It may be that this will encourage Western countries to leave the weak and failed states of the world well alone. It is not the purpose of this paper to identify contingencies for future military action. For a variety of reasons I believe that, over the medium and long term, non-intervention will be a difficult position to sustain although in the short term it may be a tempting one to try. Current exigencies may well draw Western governments into events around the globe, particularly as they affect Muslim countries. Even those aspects of contemporary conflict best handled by the police and intelligence services raise questions of strategy and the legitimacy of action.

This sets the context for the four core themes of this paper. The first is the difficulty the US armed forces face in shifting their focus from preparing for regular wars, in which combat is separated from civil society, to irregular wars, in which combat is integrated with civil society. Second, the political context of contemporary irregular wars requires that the purpose and practice of Western forces be governed by liberal values. This is also the case with regular wars, to the extent that they occur, but it is the integration with civil society that makes the application of liberal values so challenging. Third, the paper argues that this challenge becomes easier to meet when military operations are understood to contribute to the development of a compelling narrative about the likely course and consequence of a conflict, in which these values are shown to be respected. Fourth, while it is vital that the employment of armed force remains sensitive at all times to the underlying political context and to the role of narratives in shaping this context, a key test of success will always be the defeat of the opposing forces. The application of this test in regular war remains straightforward; this is not the case in irregular war, which can be of long duration and contain frequent shifts in tempo and focus. These themes raise issues that go beyond those connected with the 'war on terror', although this has undoubtedly highlighted their main features and associated dilemmas. Together they set the terms for contemporary strategic thinking.

Strategy

The concept of strategy that underpins this paper is closely related to the concept of power, understood as the ability to produce intended effects. Power is often discussed simply as capacity, normally based on military or economic strength, but in the face of certain challenges or in the pursuit of particular objectives much of this capacity may be useless. It takes strategy to unleash the power inherent in this capacity and to direct it towards specific purposes. Strategy is about choice. It depends on the ability to understand situations and to appreciate the dangers and opportunities they contain. The most talented strategists are able to look forward, to imagine quite different and more benign situations from those that currently obtain and what must be done to reach them, as well as more malign situations and how they might best be prevented. In so doing they will always be thinking about the choices available to others and how their own endeavours might be thwarted, frustrated or even reinforced. It is this interdependence of choice that provides the essence of strategy and diverts it from being mere long-term planning or the mechanical connection of available means to set ends. To focus on strategy is to emphasise the importance of choice and the extent to which the development of the international system will be much more than a function of impersonal trends or structural logic. In this respect, the transformation of strategy refers to the changing conditions in which choices must be made. While strategic discourse has now moved well beyond its etymological roots in the art of generals, and is notably prominent in organisational and business theory, this paper sticks close to the classical usage. This requires consideration of the changing character of armed forces, in terms of the development of military capabilities and the prevalent forms of conflict that shape their distribution and application.

The link with other forms of power comes at the level of grand strategy, at which the military instrument must be assessed in relation to all the other instruments available to states – economic, social and political. This is evident, for example, in the debate over the relative merits of 'hard' versus 'soft' power and the claim that in the contemporary international environment influence is as likely to flow through cultural and economic relationships as military ones. Even when it comes to military affairs, wider socio-economic and technological changes have a major impact. Indeed discussions about changes in military affairs are as likely to focus on these factors as much as the changing nature of conflict.

Strategy has traditionally been concerned with attempts by states to influence both their position within the international system and the structure of the system itself. Over past decades, changes in the international system have resulted in important developments in thinking about military strategy, for example the rise and fall of wars of decolonisation, the fixation with nuclear deterrence and the revival of interest in conventional warfare. The reasons for suggesting that a transformation of strategy is now underway reflect the demilitarisation of inter-state relations, particularly among the great powers, and the expansion of the state system as a result of decolonisation, which has resulted in many new states that are also internally unstable. Often this instability leads to violence and brings irregular forces into being. Foreign governments must then decide whether to become involved in helping to restabilise the situation or to mitigate the consequences of failing to do so. These are difficult choices and the way that they have been made and implemented has also contributed to the transformation of strategy. A further twist has been added by the arrival of super-terrorism as a major security threat and the campaign led by the Bush administration to deal directly with those responsible for past acts of terrorism and potentially for future acts. The 'war on terror', and also the more altruistic humanitarian interventions, require the separation of militants from their potential sources of support, which means understanding and, if possible, influencing the civil societies from whence they come.

Transformation

I addressed these issues in a 1998 *Adelphi Paper* entitled *The Revolution in Strategic Affairs*.[4] In it I challenged the view that a technology-driven revolution in military affairs (RMA) was underway. Although some important changes had taken place in the way that the armed forces were able to go about their business, largely the result of advances in information and communication technologies, their impact on the actual conduct of war depended on the interaction of these developments with changes of a quite different type – in political affairs – which pointed away from the decisive clash between great powers. The RMA focused on major wars like those of the past, involving regular armed forces that would benefit from technological enhancements. This paid insufficient attention to the wars that might actually have to be fought, which were more likely to be asymmetrical and irregular. This was because there was a revolution in political affairs underway that was at least as important as a revolution in military affairs. Together they could (if this language were to be employed) constitute a revolution in strategic affairs.

In some respects events since 1998 have vindicated this analysis, but there are others in which it needs to be brought up to date, notably with regard to the 'global war on terror' and the experiences of Kosovo, Afghanistan and Iraq. This *Adelphi Paper*, picking up on the themes of its predecessor, argues for thinking about the role of armed force in the light of changing political conditions and not just the new configurations made possible by the latest technological advances and organisational concepts.

CHAPTER ONE

Networks, Culture and Narratives

Since Carl von Clausewitz borrowed the concept of the 'centre of gravity' from Newtonian physics, referring to the point in a body about which it will balance, it has served as a metaphor for ways in which a well-aimed offensive thrust might knock the enemy sideways.[1] Clausewitz, considering regular war, wondered not only about the centre of gravity of an army in battle but of a whole nation. He could claim that if a nation depends on its army for protection, then the army is the nation's centre of gravity. But what if the nation were as dependent upon an alliance or on suppressing insurrectionists? Might these not also be centres of gravity? Clausewitz thought that indeed they could be and so extended the metaphor to the point where it became critically misleading and far too mechanically applied – especially by his later imitators. The term has now become used as a synonym for any potentially decisive vulnerability. Because every body must have a centre of gravity so then, it is assumed, must every army or every society. All that has to be done is to identify and to attack this centre.

In the 1980s air forces were taken up with the metaphor and spent much time discussing where the centre might be found and how it could then be targeted accurately, as if the centre of gravity of a state, and even a whole society, might be found in a collection of buildings or key facilities. Since then the vital centre has come to be identified in terms of information networks and, more recently, culture. This chapter first describes the recent development of official American strategic thinking and then considers the influence of ideas of 'network-centric' and 'culture-centric' warfare. It concludes by identifying the concept of a strategic narrative as an analytical device.

The revolution in military affairs

To understand the transformation that has taken place in military thinking a useful starting point is the 1991 Gulf War. This appeared to be a classic of manoeuvre warfare, confirming the validity of military preferences by being fought successfully along wholly conventional lines. The enemy was disoriented by means of highly mobile firepower, made possible by technical superiority and skilful orchestration of professional forces. It reflected ideas that had been under development since the late 1970s, marked in 1982 by the adoption of the doctrine of AirLand Battle, in preparation for the great confrontation between the Warsaw Pact and NATO. The renewed emphasis on manoeuvre was an explicit criticism of what was said to have been an excessive prior preoccupation with attrition. Reviving the operational arts also meant reviving ideas, going back to the aftermath of First World War, of how warfare might be rescued from the terrible consequences of attrition, in which victory required staying power above all else, as the opposing forces slogged it out, with casualties accumulating, treasury reserves depleted, industry pushed to full stretch and society becoming more fragile. The new approach was to consider the battlefield in the round. The critical attributes of successful operations were stressed as 'initiative, depth, agility and sychronization'.[2]

In 1991 the coalition, led by the United States, and including strong British and some French participation, fought along NATO lines against an opponent that had been prepared, though not very well, to fight along Warsaw Pact lines. The success of *Operation Desert Storm* convinced the military that they were thinking along the right lines. Indeed, up to this point the operational possibilities of improvements in sensors, smart weapons and systems integration were untested hypotheses. There had been talk of a renaissance in conventional strategy in the early 1970s when these new technologies first made themselves felt and this continued until the last years of the Cold War as strategies were sought that could reduce dependence on nuclear deterrence. It remained hard to imagine the scenarios, however, in which the efficacity of these strategies could be proven. Under Cold War conditions, there would always be the possibility, if a conventional battle were being lost, of escalation to nuclear exchange. Little in American military practice, up to 1991, gave cause for great confidence. The best arguments seemed to be with the sceptics, who warned of how the most conceptually brilliant systems would be brought down low by their own exceedingly complex designs, inept maintenance, incompetent operators or simply employment in climactic or topographical settings for which they were not intended. The pre-*Desert Storm* debate in the US featured many worries about the effects of sand and desert sun on equipment, predictions of high casualties in 'blue-on-blue' attacks and malfunctioning indicators leading coalition units to inflict as much damage on each other as on the enemy. These negative expectations, which may well have encouraged Saddam Hussein to risk a war with the United States, underestimated the seriousness with which the American military leadership had addressed the deficiencies exhibited in Vietnam and the promise offered by the new technologies.

First and foremost, therefore, the revolution resulting from the Gulf War was one of expectations. Up to 1991, the Americans seemed to have lost their grip on the art of warfare; after *Desert Storm* they appeared to be unbeatable – at least when fighting on their own terms. For this reason, one of the most impressive aspects of *Desert Storm* was that sufficient equipment worked as advertised to bamboozle Iraqi forces. There were compelling demonstrations of precision guidance – most dramatically in the images of 'smart' bombs entering command centres or of the *Tomahawk* cruise missile, fired from an old battleship converted for the purpose 1,000 kilometres away, navigating its way through the streets of Baghdad, entering its target by the front door and then exploding. Targets were, generally, chosen with care and, generally, attacked with confidence and minimal civilian casualties.[3]

Because the Gulf War was so one-sided, it displayed the potential of modern military systems in a most flattering light. It was as if Saddam Hussein had been asked to organise his forces in such a way as to offer coalition countries the opportunity to show off their own forces to their best advantage. A battle plan unfolded that followed the essential principles of Western military practice against a totally out-classed and out-gunned enemy who had conceded command of the air. There were no chronic deficiencies in either resources or logistics – only some unseasonable weather. The result, as noted in the *Gulf War Air Power Survey*, was not 'merely ... a conducive environment for the successful application of Western-style air power' but 'circumstances ... so ideal as to approach being the best that could be reasonably hoped for in any future conflict'.[4] This limited the extent to which formal doctrines, staff training, procurement policies and so on were truly validated, though not the extent to which they were deemed to have been so.

Proposals for future force structure built on what had worked well in ejecting Iraqi forces from Kuwait in 1991. This was the origin of the RMA, which had a number of influential proponents in the Pentagon. This assumed a technological dynamic that promised the eventual domination of the 'information environment' and thereby the 'battlespace', a term upgraded from the earlier 'battlefield' to capture the idea of combat in three dimensions. The RMA would involve a marriage of information and communications systems with those that apply military force. The potential fruits of this marriage would reflect the quality of the information that it was increasingly possible to collect, assess and transmit virtually instantaneously. The resulting combination of speed and accuracy with which force could then be applied, was described as the 'system of systems', making it possible to attack discrete though distant targets with ever greater care and precision under ever more reliable command and control.[5] While enemy commanders were still attempting to mobilise their resources and to develop their plans, they would be rudely interrupted by decisive and lethal blows inflicted by American forces for whom time and space were no longer serious constraints, leaving the enemy shocked and disabled. There was thus a move away from the crude elimination of enemy forces to more subtle notions of putting them in a position where resistance would be futile, by being able to act more quickly and to move more deftly.

The promise was particularly great for land forces. While navies and air forces had long shown how they could operate in this way, armies had traditionally sought to occupy territory and not just to eliminate items upon it. For those concerned about casualties and long-term commitments, however, ground forces are key. Infantrymen make up around 80% of US combat deaths in recent conflicts, even though they account for just 4% of the total force.[6] For some time, US military thinking has been devoted to finding ways of prevailing on land without excessive risk. RMA advocacy argued that as they took ground, the armies could manage without having their own firepower beside them, even when on the defensive, and instead rely on artillery and aircraft deployed well to their rear. Relieved of the need to travel accompanied by heavy armour and artillery, they should then be far lighter and more mobile and able to dispense with a long logistic tail. With more manpower kept to the rear, less would be at risk. In this way, warfare would move away from mass slaughter to something more contained and discriminate, geared towards disabling an enemy's military establishment with the minimum necessary force. No more resources should be expended, assets ruined or blood be shed than absolutely necessary to achieve specified political goals.

Transformation and the QDR
During the administration of President George W. Bush the theme of revolution was displaced by that of 'transformation', with Secretary of Defense

Donald Rumsfeld acting as its champion. Rumsfeld's conviction that the armed forces had become too cumbersome, geared to fighting an enemy that was unlikely to materialise while increasingly unsuited to fighting those who might, came to be reflected more in operational than budgetary terms. The wars in Afghanistan and Iraq provided an opportunity to demonstrate what could be achieved by relatively small and light forces enjoying air superiority. Given the prevailing balance of forces it was possible for American commanders to fight somewhat ad hoc campaigns, taking advantage of opportunities for breakthroughs as they arose. The ease with which the conventional stages of the battle were passed reinforced Rumsfeld's view that speed and flexibility were key to effective combat. Unfortunately, however, this method worked far less well with the next stage of bringing security to the country and defeating the various forms of resistance to the occupying powers that soon emerged.

The impact of both bureaucratic inertia and operational experience on transformation efforts is evident in the February 2006 *Quadrennial Defense Review Report* (QDR).[7] It has become a common complaint that the term 'transformation' describes a process rather than a destination and that the QDR's meditations on the implications of an age of uncertainty and surprises and calls for flexibility and adaptability indeed suggest disorientation more than a strategy. A further complaint is that despite Rumsfeld's own bold talk of major structural changes in the defence budget (now coming in at $500 billion), more than a decade of discussion of a less platform-centred approach to warfare, and a stress on lighter forces more appropriate to contemporary conditions, the US defence budget is still dominated by platforms. Rumsfeld has been no more successful than his predecessors in turning the armed services away from the 'big ticket' systems of aircraft, warships and armoured vehicles that would only really be necessary in the event of a major war against a far more substantial enemy than can currently be identified. Recognition of new strategic challenges is indicated in the pledges to 'beef up' Special Forces, to increase by a third the number of personnel specialising in psychological operations and civil affairs and to spend more on Unmanned Aerial Vehicles (UAVs).

Nonetheless, the 2006 QDR demonstrates considerable movement in US thinking since 2001. While no mistakes are acknowledged, there is an implicit recognition that the US military, and particularly the army, must make a greater effort to come to terms with irregular warfare, especially in the face of 'dispersed, global terrorist networks that exploit Islam to advance radical political aims'. The talk now is of a 'long war'.[8] The thrust of the QDR is the extent of the transformation required of US forces in response to the new strategic environment. Instead of worrying about a single, predictable and therefore deterrable state it is now necessary to address complex and unpredictable challenges, some of the most dangerous emanating from non-state actors who may well be found, and thus engaged, within countries with which the US is not actually at war. The QDR presumes the need to act before rather than after situations have reached crisis point and with 'a wartime sense of urgency'. So the option of pre-emption, highlighted so boldly in the president's 2002 *National Security Strategy*,[9] is still implied but there is now less confidence in the idea that a developing threat can be eliminated in anticipation by a bold stroke. Instead the talk is of the need of a surge capacity to meet the different types of threat as they arise.

The QDR describes four categories of problems and suggests that they require distinctive types of forces. Defeating terrorist networks thus demands Special Forces; defending the homeland in depth involves better forms of detection and protection; shaping the choices of countries at strategic crossroads will be helped by traditional mixes of conventional and nuclear forces to remind them of the wisdom of avoiding the path of confrontation; and preventing hostile states and non-state actors from acquiring or using weapons of mass destruction may require complex packages of military and non-military capabilities. The underlying theme of the document, however, is less a matter of gearing capabilities to specific problems but a fundamental shift in attitude. Planning cannot be a leisurely process geared to possible threats, but must instead be fast moving and adaptive, geared to real threats. Forces can no longer be allowed simply to reflect the distinctive institutional preferences of the single services and be maintained in a static, hollow form, only to be filled should a need arise. Instead they should be complete, integrated and ready to move, but also flexible and tailored to the crisis at hand, with powerful operational teeth and the shortest possible logistical tail. Instead of a dominant focus on major conventional combat operations it is now necessary to prepare for 'multiple irregular, asymmetric operations'. Although one might not guess from the actual budgetary commitments, these require less of an 'emphasis on ships, guns, tanks and planes' and less concern about amassing forces to engage in set-piece manoeuvres, judged by their kinetic impact. There must be more of an emphasis on 'massing effects', drawing more on 'information, knowledge and timely, actionable intelligence'.

War: 'network-centred' or 'culture-centred'?

Arguably the most important single proposition influencing contemporary American strategic thought in both official and unofficial circles is the identification of information as the key factor in military operations. It derives from a conviction that a new stage in some historically defined, and often technologically determined, sequence has been reached. The information age has been identified as the successor to the agricultural and industrial ages, bringing with it fundamental changes in the organisation of all human affairs, including the use of purposive violence.[10]

Information, once in electronic form, is unlike any other commodity: it is easy to generate, to transmit, to collect and to store. Incalculable amounts are now pumped out daily on to the internet to a near-infinite number of potential recipients with no expectation of payment and only occasional requests for user registration. 'Blogs', message boards and email contacts bring together individuals with at least one thing in common, despite many other differences. The problems this creates are those of superfluity and overload, of sorting information, identifying what is needed and distinguishing the important from the trivial and the background noise.

The tradition of worrying about information as a scarce commodity led strategists to address its growing wider importance in similar terms to other vital commodities, such as fuel and food. If information of high quality can be acquired and protected it is possible to stay ahead of opponents and competitors. Such information might include intellectual property, sensitive financial data and the plans and capabilities of government agencies and private corporations. Considerable effort goes into protecting this information from disruption or tampering and assuring its integrity. The concern lies with attack by viruses, worms, trojan horses or logic bombs,[11] often launched from distant servers for no obvious purpose but sometimes with a clear and malign intent. Criminals would be after sensitive personal details to help them to steal identities or to misappropriate funds.

Much of the early discussion on information warfare concerned these privileged information stores and flows, and the new targets being offered to wily opponents.[12] In a culture that had assumed that the best military strategies were those that caused the minimum casualties, the thought that an enemy would aim for the support systems of modern societies was both comforting and alarming at the same time.[13] The direct hurt would be slight while the indirect hurt – as transport, banking and public health systems began to break down – could be substantial. The threat gained credibility as the frequency with which companies and even high-profile networks, such as that of the US military, were attacked by a variety of hackers grew. The fear was that an enemy able to mobilise an army of software wizards could subvert an advanced society using the most insidious electronic means. But much of this was 'hacktivism', a way of making political or cultural points rather than of threatening the economy or social cohesion. Even if more determined adversaries were prepared to mount more substantial attacks the result would be likely to be 'mass disruption' rather than 'mass destruction', with inconvenience and disorientation more evident than terror and collapse.[14] These remain serious issues and considerable sums are now spent on ways of protecting and managing privileged information flows. Those involved consider themselves to be in constant battle with sophisticated foes who are persistently probing for the weakest links in networks.

A similar tendency in thinking can be observed when considering the consequences of the information age for military operations. As already remarked, the impact of the new information technologies was a key theme underlying the proclamation of the RMA. In this context the focus was on how the new technologies would affect classical forms of military operation. Its influence was evident in the 1998 paper *Joint Doctrine for Information Operations*, where information superiority was defined in largely warfighting terms, as 'the capability to collect, process, and disseminate an uninterrupted flow of information while exploiting or denying an adversary's ability to do the same'.[15] If information superiority were lost in the midst of operations the military could find air defence systems disabled, missiles sent off course, local commanders left in the dark and senior commanders confused as their screens went blank.

This view of information operations was soon challenged from two directions. It was firstly pointed out that the model for future war being proposed was one that played entirely to American strengths, including in the most advanced technologies, and for that very reason was unlikely to be embraced by the country's enemies who would be bound to look for strategies that played to American weaknesses, such as its impatience and intolerance of casualties. Such strategies came to be described as 'asymmetric', an adjective that appears regularly in the most recent QDR. This speaks to concerns that the optimum strategies for those unable to match America's conventional military capabilities (in other words, almost everyone) will be to encourage either the quagmires of irregular warfare or escalation into weapons of mass destruction. The second source of dissent came from elements in the military establishment who were dubious about the claims being made about the declining role of massed firepower and the possibility that 'information superiority' could dispel the 'fog of war'. Marine Corps Lieutenant General Paul Van Riper observed: 'Never saw and don't believe bytes of information kill enemy soldiers.' Van Riper acknowledged that improved information was helpful in supporting commanders, although he added that when this arrived as a mass of data it was of limited value.[16] The 1999 Kosovo campaign demonstrated that even with apparently complete information superiority, the fog of war had not lifted and that there were severe problems in acquiring accurate information and disseminating it effectively.[17] It was in this context that the notion of 'transformation' appeared a less ambitious and institutionally threatening concept.

The influence of the information environment then came to be seen in the ability to communicate across horizontal lines, thereby facilitating less hierarchical and flatter forms of command and control. This idea has been picked up in the notion of 'network-centred warfare'. As initially developed by Vice Admiral Arthur K. Cebrowski, US Navy, and John J. Garstka, this is geared to making battles more efficient in the same way that the application of information technology by businesses was making economies more efficient.[18] By means of 'excellent sensors, fast and powerful networks, display technology, and sophisticated modeling and simulation capabilities', information superiority could be achieved. This would mean that the force would have 'a dramatically better awareness or understanding of the battlespace rather than simply more raw data'. This could make up for deficiencies in numbers, technology or position and speed up command processes. Forces could be organised 'from the bottom up – or to self-synchronize – to meet the commander's intent'. This would lead to 'the rapid foreclosure of enemy courses of action and the shock of closely coupled events'. There would be no time for the enemy to follow the famous 'Observe–Orient–Decide–Act Loop'.[19] Even as the battle develops, situational awareness could be maintained.

Although in discussing the move from 'platform-centered' to 'network-centered' warfare, the Pentagon largely followed this formulation (Garstka was one of the authors), it also recognised that, following the physical and information domains, there was a 'cognitive domain', that of:

> the mind of the warfighter and the warfighter's supporting populace. Many battles and wars are won or lost in the cognitive domain. The intangibles of leadership, morale, unit cohesion, level of training and experience, situational awareness, and public opinion are elements of this domain. This is the domain where commander's intent, doctrine, tactics, techniques, and procedures reside.[20]

The shift to a focus on irregular warfare has had consequences for thinking about the role of information and, in particular, the cognitive domain. If the aim is to achieve a decisive victory in a regular war then information superiority will play a supplementary role, as an 'enabler', making superiority possible in the physical environment in which force is applied. In irregular warfare, superiority in the physical environment is of little value unless it can be translated into an advantage in the information environment. A sense of security, for example, is a matter of perception as much as physical fact. It has been argued that as this is the 'chosen battlespace' of its foes, the US must learn to conceptualise its victories in terms of shaping perceptions over time.[21] This fits in with the broader vision of the influence of the information age as explored by two RAND analysts, David Ronfeldt and John Arquilla. They developed the concept of 'netwars' as 'an emerging mode of conflict (and crime) at societal levels, short of traditional military warfare, in which the protagonists use network forms of organization and related doctrines, strategies, and technologies attuned to the information age'. In contrast to the large, hierarchical, stand-alone organisations that have become well established over the years and conduct police and military operations, and which extremists have often mimicked, the protagonists of netwar are 'likely to consist of dispersed organizations, small groups, and individuals who communicate, coordinate, and conduct their campaigns in an internetted manner, often without a central command'.[22]

One school of thought which draws on these insights is bound up with the view that fourth-generation warfare (4GW) has now begun. This was first developed by William Lind with a number of military colleagues.[23] According to their scheme, the first three generations had developed in response to each other (line and column, massed firepower and blitzkrieg). Into the fourth generation was carried an increasingly dispersed battlefield, reducing the importance of centralised logistics and mass (either men or firepower), and a tendency for victory to come through the implosion of the enemy rather than its physical destruction. The essence of 4GW lies in the blurring of boundaries – between war and peace, between civilian and military, between tactics and strategy, between order and chaos. Such war cannot be contained in either time or space. According to Thomas X. Hammes, such war spans the 'spectrum of human activity':

> In sum, 4GW is politically, socially (rather than technically) networked and protracted in duration. It is the anti-thesis of the high-technology, short war the Pentagon is preparing to fight.[24]

Here, the cognitive domain takes on growing importance and is influenced by far more than the speed and accuracy of information flows. There is the basis for a greater appreciation of the role of established belief systems and embedded views of the world, which helps to guide the interpretation of incoming information.

Unfortunately, whereas the RMA points to a singular form of regular warfare, which because it so suits the US is unlikely to be fought, 4GW points to almost everything else. It certainly takes in the sort of warfare in which the US is currently engaged and its influence can be seen in current views on how this should be addressed. The fact that 4GW is based on poor history, and does scant justice to the forms both regular and irregular warfare can take, is not in itself a reason for neglecting its prescriptive aspects. It is, however, important to note that the new 4GW is not usefully understood as an evolution from previous generations of warfare, as the first to third generations describe tendencies in thinking about regular battle.

The methods that are classified as 4GW are those used by the weak against the strong. Those fighting a conventionally superior capability wish to avoid direct battle in order to survive over the long term. They must find ways to demoralise the enemy while building up political support, until a tipping point is reached and the balance of power shifts decisively. This is the approach of guerrillas, resisters, partisans, insurgents, subversives, insurrectionists, revolutionaries, secessionists and terrorists and it has a long history. The methods employed by such groups are not a progression from forms of regular war, but instead constitute a parallel development. The category of 4GW is a broad one, and includes not only activities far removed from regular war but also strategies that intersect with it, either because they are complementary (for example, work with partisan groups during the Second World War) or merge into it. As the movements grow in military strength they come to embrace the methods of regular war. The generality of contemporary unconventional conflict is difficult to capture in a single category, for this is bound to miss its diversity and complex interaction with more conventional forms of warfare.

Part of the influence of 4GW theory, bolstered by recent experience, lies in the identification of 'culture' as a strategic factor in its own right as a critical influence on the cognitive dimension. Instead of the rigid empiricism of 'network-centric' warfare in its first guise, there has been an almost post-modernist embrace of pre-rational and embedded patterns of thought that allow individuals, and broad social groups, to be caught up in a particular view of the world that helps them to make sense of unfolding events, even to the point of being highly resistant to inconvenient facts. In a particularly extreme formulation, such as Lind's, culture has become the weakest strategic link, a point which the enemy can work upon to fracture American security.[25]

Major-General Robert H. Scales, Jr, in seeking to explain the contrast between the failure of Islamic armies when fighting conventional battles,

Western-style, but their far greater success in unconventional war, has developed the concept of 'culture-centric warfare'.[26] In facing an enemy that 'uses guile, subterfuge, and terror mixed with patience and a willingness to die', he argues, too much has been spent attempting to gain 'a few additional meters of precision, knots of speed, or bits of bandwidth' and too little to create a 'parallel transformation based on cognition and cultural awareness'. Winning wars requires:

> creating alliances, leveraging nonmilitary advantages, reading intentions, building trust, converting opinions, and managing perceptions—all tasks that demand an exceptional ability to understand people, their culture, and their motivation...
>
> Sensors, computer power, and bandwidth count for little against a dispersed enemy who communicates by word of mouth and back-alley messengers and fights using simple weapons that do not require networks or sophisticated technological integration to be effective.

Care is needed here. In practice, culture is less of a fixed and known quality but more an amalgam of language, tradition, religious practices and social structures, and political values. The key question is the degree to which the culture, or some element within it, has become politicised, differentiating groups from each other. It is one thing to support a national soccer team; another to feel patriotic pride at a military display; another still to be consumed with hatred of all those with an alien culture. Culture, and the cognition which it influences, is rarely fixed but in a process of development and adaptation, shaped by the encounter between received beliefs and everyday experience, and by the competing analyses and explanations provided by the print, broadcasting and web-based media.

Strategic narratives

It is in this context that the concept of narratives – compelling story lines which can explain events convincingly and from which inferences can be drawn – becomes relevant. Narratives are designed or nurtured with the intention of structuring the responses of others to developing events. They are strategic because they do not arise spontaneously but are deliberately constructed or reinforced out of the ideas and thoughts that are already current. According to Ronfeldt and Arquilla,[27] networks are held together by narratives. They emphasise that narratives go beyond rhetoric 'scripted for manipulative ends', but instead 'provide a grounded expression of people's experiences, interests, and values'. Stories both 'express a sense of identity and belonging', and 'communicate a sense of cause, purpose, and mission'. This helps a dispersed group to cohere and guides its strategy. Individuals know the sort of action expected of them and the message to be conveyed.

Narratives are about the ways that issues are framed and responses suggested. They are not necessarily analytical and, when not grounded in evidence or experience, may rely on appeals to emotion, or on suspect metaphors and dubious historical analogies. A successful narrative will link certain events while disentangling others, distinguish good news from bad tidings, and explain who is winning and who is losing. This usage reflects the idea that stories play an extremely important role in communication, including the ways that organisations talk about themselves. The notion of the narrative is already well established among strategists working in the domestic political arena, for example in guiding the activity popularly known as 'spin'. Ideas about 'controlling the agenda', keeping some big ideas to the fore and not allowing them to be crowded out by trivialities, inserting the right 'soundbites' into news bulletins, ensuring party members stay 'on message' and influencing the 'story line' reflect the view that opinions are shaped not so much by the information received but the constructs through which that information is interpreted and understood. The concept is therefore now central to the study of journalism.[28] Convincing the public that the economy is really doing well when the latest data suggest the opposite, or that the murky past of a candidate for high office is irrelevant, requires a keen sense of how the media works, from timing news announcements, both positive and negative, briefing key journalists and keeping an eye on internet 'blogs'. An effective narrative will work not only because it appeals to the values, interests and prejudices of the intended audience but also because it is not going to be exposed by later information and events.

There is nothing new in the concept that worthy causes or quality products can fail because of ineffectual communication. Intellectuals through the ages have been animated by the conviction that language and the construction of ideas matter. Contemporary interest in the matter is fuelled by the intensity and complexity of the media environment but also by an anxiety on the part of commentators that spin diminishes public discourse, assuming limited attention spans, fascination with process rather than substance, with who is up or down rather than what is right or wrong. The ability of single-issue pressure groups to convince people that anything genetically modified is dangerous or that the theory of evolution is bunkum can be seen as testament to the inability of those with cautious, moderate, analytical viewpoints to shape debates while challenged by the dramatic and sensational.

The ability to market political ideas, policies and even individual candidates should not be exaggerated. Although some stories can be sustained as matters of faith, in many cases if they are not grounded in some sort of reality they are likely to fail eventually, and those that have promulgated them will suffer a resultant loss of credibility. The more overt the spinning, the less trustworthy the source. The growing public awareness of the constancy of spin means that it has reduced underlying levels of trust in governments, despite the increased recruitment of communication specialists.

This point is particularly important when the narratives concern war. When territory is lost or armies surrender no amount of clever talk can hide the defeats. The importance of morale, at the front and to the rear, has long demanded that narratives be deployed with sensitivity, even if that term has not been used. Military strategists are grasping at it whenever they wonder how to fight the 'propaganda war' (or more euphemistically these days the 'information war') and it is implied with every reference to a battle for 'hearts and minds'. At times of major war, whole government departments are devoted to psychological warfare or what might now be called 'public affairs'. Winston Churchill's great gift as a war leader was said to be in mobilising the English language as a weapon of war, to inspire and to reassure the British people.[29] There are a number of reasons why this question of narrative has moved to the centre-stage of strategy at this time, and these reasons differ somewhat from those of the past. This is largely a function of the same media environment that is affecting domestic political life, but which is taken to extremes when armed forces are engaged in combat.

The discretionary and often controversial nature of contemporary conflicts means that they intersect in crucial ways with the domestic political debate. The 2003 Iraq War helps to explain the growing interest in the concept of the narrative in mainstream strategic studies. For the first time since Vietnam the conduct of a protracted conflict has become a major issue in American politics. Prior to the 2003 war with Iraq, the US government made assertions which were recognised at the time as being overstated and were shown later to have been quite wrong with respect to such matters as nuclear programmes and the links between Saddam Hussein and al-Qaeda.[30] As the rationale moved towards the delivery of freedom and democracy to a post-Saddam Iraq, the ability to provide a convincing narrative that explained the ferocity of the insurgency and the difficulties of nation-building became critical to the debate about whether the war had been worth the pain and cost. Within Iraq itself, the question of whether the insurgents could ever be overcome affected not only morale but also basic political decisions on how to relate to the American-backed government. The issue of Iraq in the rhetoric of US and coalition governments was couched within the terminology of the 'war on terror' – itself the subject of rigorous debate as critics argued that such language encouraged attempts at military solutions to an essentially political problem – and poorly specified the problem as being about an objection-able tactic rather than an ideology.

An important part of the narrative is the way that issues come to be framed. A common complaint of critics of war (and sometimes just those eager for a different perspective) is that the experts used by the media to explain the course of conflict tend to be a certain sort of specialist, thinking within an established framework who can only throw light on what might be considered their professional précis of why troops are being deployed in a particular way, or the capabilities of weapons systems. Jay Rosen, for example, has described his failed attempts during the 1991 Gulf War to interest TV stations in another angle. He chose the concept of a just war, how it might look from different ethical and religious perspectives, and how it might be applied in this case. No such discussion was aired. This, according to Rosen, illustrates how the media's ability to decide what to include is a choice about which concerns and voices matter. 'To put it another way, journalists make casting decisions. They decide whom to cast in what roles in the drama of public life.'[31]

One should not expect mainstream strategists to get too upset about this. After all, it is their expertise that will be deemed most relevant and they will make the media appearances. When a nation's security and pres-tige is at stake it is not surprising that the question of whether the war can be won looms larger than that of whether the war is just. Perhaps media discussions reinforce established views, but there can also be dangers if these same discussions give undue prominence to perspectives that are held only by a minority, or turn off readers and viewers because they cannot engage their interests. The point can also be made that when the 2003 war came along, questions of legitimacy were much more to the fore, certainly before it started, albeit more in the European than the American media. Once the war is underway the 'who is winning and how' questions become more salient again, but the truly tricky period comes afterwards. During a regular conflict, strategists can talk about the things they understand, such as logistics, firepower and manoeuvre. But just like a regular army, they can all of a sudden appear to be out of their depth as a conflict takes on a more irregular form. To know who is winning and who is losing, differ-ent questions need to be asked. Who is the enemy? What are they fighting for? How do these people fit into the local political structure? What sort of support do they enjoy? How do we know? What is it about 'our side' that allows them to have such a constituency? What does 'victory' mean in this context? To answer these questions requires different sorts of expertise.

For regular forces trying to cope with swarms of irregulars this raises the question of whether the narrative can provide a special focus for their efforts to disrupt the enemy. It has been argued that:

> A grand counter-terrorism strategy would benefit from a comprehensive consideration of the stories terrorists tell; understanding the narratives which influence the genesis, growth, maturation and transformation of terrorist organiza-tions will enable us to better fashion a strategy for undermining the efficacy of those narratives so as to deter, disrupt and defeat terrorist groups.[32]

The idea of the narrative therefore opens up another possibility of military operations. Instead of being geared to eliminating the assets of the enemy, they might need to be focused on undermining those narratives on which that enemy bases its appeal and which animates and guides its activists.

CHAPTER TWO

The Transformation of Grand Strategy

Liberalism is the most important expression of the political aspects of Western culture. It must therefore provide the foundation for any compelling strategic narratives, although liberalism contains a number of inherent tensions which affect the way these narratives develop. It is these tensions which provide the substance of internal Western debate over the rights and wrongs of military operations. But before discussing these tensions, it is necessary to consider the changes in the international system which have not only highlighted the importance of irregular warfare but also raised new questions about liberal values and the use of force.

Grand strategy

In traditional 'realist' views of the international system, power appears as both ends and means, measured in terms of the more blatant indicators of military and economic strength, deriving its main purpose from its own accumulation and its only validation through comparison with others. The only test of a regime claiming sovereignty over a particular territory would be that it was sovereign in practice: that it could maintain an internal order and survive war. This did not allow for challenges to a regime according to higher claims of justice or righteousness. The only challenge which mattered would be one based on power. The answer to the apparent problem that if effective power were the basis of legitimacy then superior power would always be more legitimate lay in the understanding that an unregulated anarchy would be disastrous and that therefore a form of self-regulation was necessary. Realism thus encourages the view that in vital respects the contemporary international system is not so different from that of two centuries ago and that the key changes can be charted largely with reference to those in the material foundations of power. Those at the top of the hierarchy are assumed to acquire a natural affection for the status quo and are therefore inherently conservative. They are prepared to defend their privileged position against the malcontent revisionists who want to restructure the system to give themselves pride of place.

This is a view that is easy to caricature but not to disregard. If states believe that the international system works in a particular way, and act accordingly, then this view will be constantly reinforced. Furthermore, at certain critical junctures, raw military power matters and can make all the difference. States that neglect this factor may suffer. This 'realist' view, however, remains vulnerable to the charge of being too cynical in assuming that power is all that matters, that domestic politics are irrelevant and that the individual units only relate to each other on the basis of a straightforward calculus of relative strength, varied by means of alliances and the occasional war.

In this realist tradition, grand strategy is concerned with the use by states of all available means – social, economic, political as well as military – to position themselves within the international system. Since the evaporation of the threat posed by the Soviet bloc at the end of the 1980s this has not seemed problematic: the United States and its allies have enjoyed unprecedented levels of security. It could almost be said that the problem of major war has been solved. During the early stages of the development of the state system, it was taken for granted that the natural vocation of great powers was to expand, which meant that war was likely to result from the vulnerability of small powers in the face of neighbouring predators and the constant risk of great powers colliding with each other. By the end of the twentieth century, however, all parts of the world were spoken for, with no territory up for grabs. Having disposed of their empires, the old imperial powers had little interest in taking on subject populations. This did not mean that all thoughts of mergers and acquisitions had been banished, especially in the more unsettled regions, but there were no longer competitive drives for colonies or attempts to refashion boundaries into more convenient shapes that might be easier to defend or contain more lucrative assets. Western governments were also no longer in thrall to mercantilism. Once they might have contemplated a world full of 'vital interests', in terms of colonies or trade and supply routes, but such a perspective was now outdated. Market factors became far more important than the political in determining patterns of trade and access to raw materials and in a global economic system.

The Cold War had pitted liberalism and socialism, two traditions that had emerged out of the European Enlightenment, against each other. It ended the way it did because people living under the dead hand of European communism were increasingly looking to the West for political and economic guidance. When that struggle was over, liberalism emerged triumphant. There was now not only one dominant power but also one dominant ideology, which would, in principle, result in a more manageable global order. With state socialism discredited there was no real alternative model for other states to adopt. Asian countries still claiming to be Marxist, notably China but also Vietnam, sought access to international markets.

Globalisation

Colonialism, which provided a vehicle for great power rivalry, was also profoundly illiberal in its underlying presumption. The continental empires of Eurasia – the Austro-Hungarian and the Ottoman – lacked any ideological basis for justifying their particular configuration. The Ottoman Empire had Islam, but this provided no basis for holding on to Christian provinces. They were both vulnerable to liberal sentiment else-where, particularly in Britain, objecting to the suppression of nationalist aspirations. It took, of course, some time before non-Europeans were also allowed to share these aspirations. In Africa and Asia, liberal colonisers had an extraordinary capacity to convince themselves that the subject peoples were more than happy to merge their destinies with the metropolis, or at least that they would if they had the capacity to think these destinies through for themselves.

It took the upheavals associated with the Second World War to create the conditions for full-scale decolonisation outside Europe and the Americas. The forces of nationalism made themselves felt in the 'third world' (the first two being the capitalist and socialist worlds). Initially these forces were resisted but gradually they were accommodated. The processes of decolo-nisation and the conduct of the Cold War became increasingly intertwined. In some ways they could be said to have concluded at the same time with the implosion of European communism. This resulted in the end of satellite status for central and eastern European states and the creation of 15 new states out of the Soviet Union. The fragmentation continued in Europe, with five new states emerging violently out of the former Yugoslavia and two more peacefully out of the former Czechoslovakia. At the end of the Second World War, the UN was formed with 51 member states; there are now 191. While the end of the Cold War created the potential for a more orderly world, decolonisation had left it more disorderly.

The legacy of the decolonisation process was contradictory: it simultaneously enhanced both the significance of sovereignty and the moral force of the principle of self-determination. This would not have been problematic if states were all organised on the basis of coherent, homogenous nations. Unfortunately, the concept of the 'nation-state' is often wishful thinking. Nations are created through bonds of language, religion, ethnicity and culture. States require loyalty to institutions and laws. These inherent tensions, which many states have learned to manage through a variety of constitutional devices to the point where shared identities and loyalties have been forged that transcend national differences, have often been aggravated by the deficient processes of decolonisation. Many states contain more than one nation while nations are often to be found in more than one state. A key source of contemporary global disorder in a nutshell is that people give their loyalties to nations but they are governed by states.

To the speed with which new states came into being, the lack of prior preparation for self-government and the fragile nature of the civil societies upon which they were based could often be added undeveloped economies and poverty. Undeveloped institutional structures meant that the new states were often unable to contain and channel the inevitable political tensions. Endemic instability in many new states recast the problem of order. For most of the twentieth century it was bound up with inter-state relations and particularly the challenge of persuading a number of competing great powers to co-exist without war. Now it was the result of the proliferation of states, many of which were failing in the key test of statehood by being unable to monopolise violence within their own borders.

These failures and inabilities were viewed with some concern in the West, but the inclination was not to get involved. At first, after the collapse of communism, the expectation was that liberal capitalism would advance through seduction rather than rape. Countries seeking to integrate into the global marketplace would accept the political consequences. In central and eastern Europe, for example, the prospect of membership of the European Union was the single most important factor encouraging and guiding the economic and political reforms in the post-communist states. Not only were capital, goods and services moving around the world with extraordinary speed and efficiency, but so too were the concepts and practices of the dominant actors. Gaining access to Western markets and credits required conceding ground to Western information and ideas. On this basis, the problems of world order could be resolved without effort. Market forces would bring about new types of cooperative relationships which states dare not ignore and would be wise to embrace. They would produce greater prosperity and the steady embrace of democracy, which would in turn encourage a disinclination to war.

The 1990s were certainly good economic years for Western consumers but there was no simple, single explanation for this prosperity. What was presented as a systemic shift could also be interpreted as a rather fortuitous conjunction of disparate factors. Low commodity (particularly oil) prices helped. The beneficiaries were also thinly spread: many parts of the world – notably sub-Saharan Africa – were completely excluded and instead caught in cycles of poverty and despair. The 'trickle-down effect' from the good times in the West on the rest of the world was tangible but modest. Meanwhile, the numbers afflicted by HIV/AIDS rose, as did concerns about global warming. There was evidence of remorseless demographic pressures, with populations increasingly dominated by the young, urban and unemployed. The world's population increased from 2.5 billion in 1950 to 6 billion in 2000. Within another 50 years, 60% of the world's population will live in cities. The demands on agriculture were becoming intense, aggravated by environmental degradation and the scarcity of fresh water. Under these conditions, market-based remedies were not always appropriate or sufficiently radical.

There was nothing inevitable about globalisation in the form of economic interdependence leading to more peace.[1] Countries plugged into the Western economic system did not necessarily conform to Western political values and practices. In Asia and the Middle East, the alternatives to authoritarianism and repression often presented themselves more in anarchic or totalitarian forms than as democracy (and that was certainly the view of many of the regimes in question). Western hegemony was treated with suspicion. While much commercial and financial activity was conducted by entities which enjoyed significant autonomy and were not beholden even to those states which hosted their headquarters, they were largely and unmistakably Western in character. However diverse and pluralistic the world seemed to Western eyes, and however irrelevant twentieth-century concerns about great power struggles appeared, to non-Western eyes the world was being shaped by a group of victorious great powers seeking to impose an ideological hegemony of their own, which demonstrated a low tolerance of any opposition. Because the attempted ideological hegemony was liberal in both economic and political terms, it was neither as repressive nor aggressive as the attempted Nazi or communist hegemonies it defeated, and could make a more impressive empirical case that it was underpinned by convincing economic and social theory.

Nonetheless, it could still appear threatening to those whose local order had more illiberal roots and who were culturally resistant to what was considered in the West to be political and economic 'best practice'.

In the West, an opportunity for restricting the role of the state (but maintaining its capacity to regulate the private sector for the collective good) could, if applied in less developed countries, lead to the growth in power of the shadowy and unaccountable, from groups with bizarre ideologies to those settling ethnic scores, from warlords to organised crime. Without an effectively functioning state, political freedoms may start to appear to be meaningless: economic power can become one sided to the point where individuals feel bereft of real choice and attempts to express the collective will are readily subverted through corrupt practices. In all societies, ultimate power depends on the control of the means of organised violence – the police and the armed forces. Here there are limits to any re-balancing of the relationship between the state, individuals and other socio-political groups. It remains the case that the most fundamental challenge a state can face – internally as well as externally – is to its monopoly of organised violence, reflected in gang warfare or civil war as much as external war, and the acquisition of military capabilities by illegitimate groups at home as well as hostile powers abroad. The most important challenges for international order come from places where this capacity for internal order has been lost.

Weakness and failure in the non-Western world have consequences for Western states: sudden population movements; environmental disasters; local conflicts being exported through expatriate communities. Even before the emergence of jihadist terrorism as the top priority for Western security agencies in 2001, there were links between the degree of disorder in particular countries and the quality of Western life. This could manifest itself in the production and distribution of hard drugs for Western markets or refugees from conflicts adding to the strain on local communities when they turned up as asylum seekers. International criminal organisations grew in power and influence as a direct consequence of economic and trade liberalisation and the opportunities provided by modern telecommunications and information systems. Those trafficking in people, drugs, arms and precious goods became much more sophisticated in their manipulation of the financial system, taking opportunities for political corruption and fuelling conflicts. Gangsters shaped not only criminal networks but almost parallel political systems, sometimes with their own armed forces. This activity was not always necessarily of a disorderly nature. Such arrangements could involve clear lines of authority and enforced rules – it was just that there was only a scant relationship to formal governmental structures. In many countries, in combination with fragile state structures, crime as big business became a political as well as an economic force to be reckoned with. Moreover, politically extreme groups with a propensity for violent action often interacted naturally with criminal networks. New, shadowy centres of power emerged requiring as much attenion as radical and delinquent states.

This is not to argue for the proclamation of a systemic shift in a more malign direction, instead of more positive notions of globalisation. It is probably best to avoid the simplistic drawing of trend lines in either optimistic or pessimistic directions. The more persuasive conclusion is that Western governments have difficult choices to make about how they look after their own people and act beyond their borders.

American grand strategy

With the end of the Cold War not only was the US confirmed at the top of the hierarchy but so also was its ideology. This was first evident in great power relations. There were no longer ideological struggles fuelling great power competition. According to the accepted nostrums of realist international theory, the first priority of its security policy must be to hold on to that position. The leaked *Defense Planning Guidance* of 1992 described the first objective of the United States as 'to prevent the re-emergence of a new rival, either on the territory of the former Soviet Union or elsewhere, that poses a threat on the order of that posed formerly by the Soviet Union'. This carried through to a determination to prevent any 'hostile power from dominating a region whose resources would, under consolidated control, be sufficient to generate global power'.[2]

Realist scholars searched for potential revisionists, with the candidates not always confined to the overtly hostile: a united Germany was identified, as was the economically dynamic Japan.[3] In the event both countries, having made the case during previous decades for the possibility of international strength based largely on economic rather than military power, entered a period of stagnation and fell back in the power stakes. Even if they had not it was by no means obvious on what basis they would mount an overt challenge to American primacy, from which they had both benefited over the previous four decades. Thereafter, China came to be written about in terms similar to those once reserved for Japan, with an expectation that its fast-growing economic strength would continue unabated (despite developing environmental, social and political problems) and would soon be translated into military capacity to be followed by increasingly aggressive political demands.[4]

Official America has been careful when it comes to identifying major countries, with whom it is attempting to have cooperative relations, as potential threats. The 2006 QDR refers to a category of states (including China but also Middle Eastern countries) at a 'strategic crossroads'. They are to be encouraged to think of the most positive route to follow by having their attention drawn to the substantial US military strength that they might have to confront should they choose the most negative. Whether or not these countries really consider themselves to be at a strategic crossroads, facing definitive choices about their future international alignments and aspirations, this formulation at least acknowledges that they are not yet set in their ways.

At the same time, American power, and the political, economic and cultural hegemony that can flow from it, inevitably generates anxiety and various forms of resistance around the world. The problem for those who might want to act as a counterweight to it is that they lack the raw strength, certainly individually but also collectively, to do so. In addition, they are not invariably in opposition to the generality of American foreign policy. The most thorough study of the problem of why American primacy makes other states anxious and how they respond to it demonstrates that real constraints on American foreign policy can emerge from these responses, but also the diversity of forms they can take, from sullen resistance to active accommodation as well as conscious balancing.[5] In traditional, inter-state terms, attempts to organise countervailing power have been somewhat half-hearted. For example, those who intended to provide a counterweight to American policy around the time of the 2003 Iraq War foundered on the varying agendas of the members (Russia, China, France and occasionally Germany) and their lack of fundamental differences with the United States.

In fact the diplomatic rows, in particular in the run-up to the 2003 war, were intense largely because the experience from the end of the Cold War up to this point had suggested that there was a sufficient consensus among the great powers, and in particular the five permanent members of the UN Security Council, to enable the UN to function. A big boost had occurred to the organisation's standing in 1990–91 when it served as the focal point for international opposition to Iraq's occupation of Kuwait and was asked to give its blessing to military action. This was a case of a lesser, though still substantial, state challenging the status quo through a clear act of aggression. Soviet support was achieved by working through the Security Council. President George H.W. Bush hailed this approach as evidence of a 'new world order', although actually it was more a revived old order. The new understanding between Moscow and Washington allowed the UN Security Council to work at last as originally intended.[6] The justifications for Kuwait's forceful liberation derived less from liberal values than from traditional concepts of security and order. Iraq had challenged a basic principle of international order – non-aggression. Building the coalition to liberate Kuwait required honouring the other core norm of non-interference in internal affairs.

Yet while this fitted in with their self-perception as upholders of the international status quo, the new configurations of power meant that the erstwhile status quo powers of the West found themselves occupying the position of the radicals, subverting disagreeable regimes and demanding changes in inefficient economic practices. This hegemony, however, could not be an effortless development, as the enthusiasts for globalisation hoped, as events moved inexorably in their direction simply because of the proven superiority of their political and economic structures. If they could only feel adequately secure through the construction of a global liberal order they were going to find it hard work. Instead of yesterday's 'troublespots' progressively turning into today's 'emerging markets', it soon became apparent that a more likely prospect was of a patchy and controversial process whereby the leading Western states combined to bring a modicum of stability to areas of conflict, often on an emergency basis, using economic and military means. So the spread of the Western model was as likely to depend on deliberate and determined political action as much as on osmosis or market forces. Meanwhile, a substantial proportion of the world's population would continue to live in a distressed state for some time to come and this distress could be aggravated by political disorder or result in such disorder.

Liberal wars

All societies expect to fight their wars according to the core values upon which they are based. In the case of Western countries this must mean liberal values, though the term 'liberal' can have a number of potential meanings, not all of them helpful. It can, for example, imply support from only one part of the political spectrum and not necessarily the most important part. In the United States the term is often used as a synonym for 'leftist' or even 'socialist'. In Europe, where the term has different ideological implications, the lack of liberalism in contemporary America is often criticised. In practice, however, as I have demonstrated elsewhere, political debate on both sides of the Atlantic draws on classical liberal values.[7] These values provide the philosophical underpinnings of all Western states, defining the essence of a good society with their focus on individualism, civil and political liberties, the rule of law, the consent of the governed and opposition to arbitrary authority. These values have survived challenges from totalitarian and authoritarian regimes and movements of many complexions. Liberal ideology inspired the transatlantic states in two world wars and the Cold War. Its victories in these confrontations explains why these states do not now experience serious forms of existential threat from other great powers. Those states that might challenge their ascendancy in economic or political terms, for example China, lack the basis for an internationalist ideological appeal. Liberalism remains a potent force because it does have such appeal. When Western governments deviate from these principles they can expect heavy domestic criticism in response. So they will always seek to demonstrate that their actions are perfectly compatible with them. It may be that future political developments will divert Western countries away from these principles, influenced perhaps by religious fundamentalism, racism or extreme nationalism but, although tendencies exhibiting these alternative philosophies are evident, they are far from likely to refashion Western political life.

There are two different types of difficulty with the term 'liberal' that are much more serious. The first points to a familiar tension in the liberal tradition, between upholding the core values of individualism and liberty, even when they are disruptive and inconvenient, and a yearning for the conditions of relative calm and order in which liberal values are more likely to thrive. The second points to the very idea of a liberal war as oxymoronic: war has an inherently illiberal quality. Wars are arbitrary and unpredictable in their effects, ruining and cutting short many lives and imposing great sacrifices on others. They require the suppression of individuality and the qualification of civil liberties in pursuit of the collective good. They invoke, in prospect and practice, the rawest human emotions, almost always including fear and chronic insecurity, as well as greed and protectiveness toward others, heroism and cruelty. Plans may be hatched by the cool and the calculating, but they are likely to be implemented by the passionate and the unpredictable. Because Western liberal societies recoil at these inherent characteristics of war, they have recoiled at war itself, and when it appears to be unavoidable they have sought to render it more rational and controllable.

Historically, liberalism has been associated internationally with the attempt to find an answer to the problem of war by encouraging benign socio-economic developments that undermine nationalism, enlightened dispute settlement and strong international institutions. Yet it has also developed as a response to the problem of injustice and the denial of political rights. The tension between the strand of liberalism that is antimilitarist and anxious to find peaceful forms of dispute resolution and the strand that abhors injustice and repression is captured by the norm of non-interference in internal affairs, which can be presented both as a vital principle of international order and a charter for domestic repression, and is thrown into relief when challenges arise from illiberal ideologies that show scant respect for either human rights or international law and institutions. The tension between the two strands of liberalism as they tried to solve the problems of war and injustice together was well described by Michael Howard in *War and the Liberal Conscience*. It is worth quoting his conclusion at length. The liberal tradition, he wrote:

> has certainly been a tradition often marred by naiveté, by intellectual arrogance, by ignorance, by confused thinking and sometimes, alas, by sheer hypocrisy. But how can one fail to share the aspirations of those who carried on in this tradition, or deny credit to their achievements? It is thanks to the patient work, over nearly two centuries, of the men and women who have been inspired by the liberal conscience that so much progress has been made in the creation of a global community of nations; that values are today asserted as universal to which all states without exception pay at least lip service; that it is recognised even if only in principle that states have communal obligations and duties within a freely-accepted framework of international society. The danger lies in forgetting that each actor in this society of states, including those who have not yet achieved statehood, embodies distinct cultural perceptions and values; that it is ultimately concerned quite inevitably and properly with its own survival; and that it is unwilling, whatever declarations may be made to the contrary, totally to rely on the power and the will of the international community as a whole to protect it.[8]

In international relations theory, liberalism is still associated with an optimistic view of the possibilities of taming the international system's anarchic and unruly character by encouraging economic interdependence, reliance on reason and goodwill in managing crises and conflicts and institutional innovation at the supranational level. It seeks to encourage states to rely less on 'hard' military power and more on 'soft' forms,[9] including cultural appeal, diplomatic clout, positions in international organisations and the capacity to dole out economic and technical assistance. One consequence of this preoccupation with the problem of war has been to encourage measures, such as disarmament or respect for the fragile claims of international law, that reduce the capacity to implement purely national strategies in response to international challenges.

Accepting that the dangers inherent in the international system can be mitigated by insisting that all states respect each other's sovereignty can also mean accepting the potentially illiberal subordination of the rights of individuals and groups to those of states. In this respect, an anxiety to prevent war can mean playing down ideological differences, for example with suggestions that the sources of conflict are likely to be found in misperceptions and miscalculations, often aggravated through arms races. For these reasons, internationalist approaches are likely to work best when there is not so much wishful thinking but genuinely a greater underlying consensus and a readiness to avoid bringing conflicts to a head. The effort to avoid war while ensuring respect for the sovereignty of all states tends to be more manageable when there is a common ideological basis for the exercise of power within individual states. The original Treaty of Westphalia of 1648, which established the primacy of sovereignty and non-interference in internal affairs, was about preventing future clashes between Protestant and Catholic countries over the composition of each other's regimes. After the Napoleonic Wars, the victorious powers sought to manage the system through a set of rules which essentially conservative states should have had no difficulty in following when regulating their relations. They were wary of any revolutionary ideology which provided not only a catalyst for the accumulation of power and territory but also contested their own legitimacy. Such gatherings as the Congress of Vienna in 1815, the League of Nations in 1919 and the United Nations in 1945 followed the defeat of threatening ideologies – in turn revolutionary republicanism, anti-democratic authoritarianism and racist nationalism. Each time, the hope was that a new consensus could be based on a set of shared principles. They failed when new ideological fault-lines opened up.[10]

Attempts to establish the rule of international law, and even to move towards world government, assumed that these could be founded upon the core principles of liberalism, depending upon the right to liberty at the individual level and self-determination at the national. So long as there was mutual respect for these rights then there was no problem. The challenge for international order, as with domestic order, was to ensure that the community as a whole protected these rights against those who sought to deny them. This carried two difficulties. First, liberalism, taken seriously, is subversive and thus inherently disorderly. Second, it must include a basic freedom to ignore the problems of others and this makes it difficult to develop a theory of political obligation, which is essential if great powers are to take responsibility for international order. Liberalism provides no rationale for interfering with the attempts of self-defining political units to create their destinies just so long as they do not interfere unduly with the destinies of others.

Defensive and offensive liberal wars

The pressures to get involved and to address developments within states that pose a challenge to the liberal conscience, can be described as a move from *defensive* to *offensive* liberal wars. The defensive types are undertaken in the face of threats to liberal values. On this basis, the two world wars and the Cold War of the last century were liberal wars, at least for the transatlantic powers. So, in some respects, is the 'war on terror'.[11] In these cases, liberalism defines the ideological stakes involved in these conflicts, what it is the Western democracies believe they are fighting for. Such wars are wholly consistent with the principle of non-interference in internal affairs, especially as it is liberal affairs that are the target of the interference. *Offensive* liberal wars, by contrast, challenge this principle. These are designed to bring liberal values to parts of the world where they are not yet in evidence. For that reason they tend to focus on the balance of power within states rather than between states and reflect the growing importance of the norms of human and minority rights. This means that almost by definition they challenge the norm of non-interference in internal affairs.

The possible existence of a category of military operations that involved working within other states rather than against them became evident in the immediate aftermath of the 1991 Gulf War. When the Kurds to the north and the Shi'ites to the south rebelled against the Iraqi regime they were ruthlessly suppressed. The coalition did nothing. As fleeing Kurds were caught on the borders between Iraq and Turkey (which would not let them enter), and with the international media, still in the area after the war, reporting on the terrible hardships they suffered, the coalition countries accepted that perhaps the internal affairs of Iraq had become their business. UN Security Council Resolution 688 of April 1991 deplored the repression and, while it did not authorise any action at all, the sentiment it expressed was taken as a form of authority for the establishment of a safe haven in northern Iraq, initially protected by coalition forces. This set a precedent for future humanitarian interventions. The most important events in terms of forcing governments to address the problems of humanitarian intervention were the wars of the Yugoslav dissolution. After the short but barely contested secession of Slovenia in June 1991, the other wars were vicious and marked by the forcible eviction of populations – so-called ethnic cleansing – to redraw political borders. Croatia, Bosnia and Kosovo set the developing terms for intervention in the internal affairs of states behaving badly. Out of this came the new dispensation that, in exceptional circumstances, major powers could ignore the norm of non-interference.

The 'international community', to the extent that its views were expressed through the UN Security Council, increasingly expected its members to uphold the basic rights of individuals and minorities. A high-level group of academics and former practitioners produced a report, called *The Responsibility to Protect*, deliberately over-turning the old presumption of a responsibility to stay out. [12] This reflected a growing reluctance to turn a blind eye to crude forms of repression and persecution for the sake of a quiet life. 'Human security' emerged as a set of requirements to be set against those of national and international security. This was connected to evidence of repression, social breakdown and the manifold deprivations and depravities associated with civil war. There were other more self-interested reasons for getting involved: because expatriate communities were at risk or pernicious and repressive ideologies were taking root; because, left unregulated, such conflicts could encourage crime and various forms of trafficking in drugs, arms or people; or else because they might spread, so that a whole region might be dragged down, resulting in refugee flows, interrupted trade and general mayhem. The nearer to home the greater these dangers, which is why neighbouring powers were more likely to intervene in regional conflicts (Russia in its 'near abroad', the US in Haiti, West Europeans in the former Yugoslavia, Australia in East Timor). These factors also help to explain why, except where there were historic links (as with Britain in Sierra Leone), intervention in Africa proved to be so problematic.

Furthermore, interventions created new interests. The reputations of the intervening countries and the sponsoring multilateral organisation (if any) would be affected by their performance in the conflict and their ability to get results. It took most of the 1990s, for example, for the idea of an active European foreign policy to recover from the dismal failure of the first attempts to forge one in the context of the break-up of Yugoslavia early in the decade. At the same time, non-intervention could also have an effect on reputation and encourage others subsequently to disregard the non-intervener's concerns when pursuing their own particular quarrels. Nonetheless, the impact of a decision to admit failure and to withdraw was always likely to be far more significant than holding back in the first place.[13]

This trend was not without its critics in the West. Jurists were anxious about the challenge posed to the principle of non-interference while governments saw dangers of being pressed into costly and hazardous interventions. Media pressure was often blamed, as if by highlighting human distress and political abuses it could move governments to take action in areas where prudence might otherwise have held them back. When moral imperatives drive foreign policy there are risks of double standards and unintended consequences. Once the rights of states do not take precedence then all demands for self-determination must be taken seriously, even where groups are not suffering evident persecution and denial of political opportunities, or where it is hard to see how they could realistically lead to viable state-hood, or where the satisfaction of one group would inevitably raise exactly the same demands from others who might fear becoming disadvantaged minorities within the new states. Russia and China, as the most important states on the edges of the Western system and willing participants in the international economy, were concerned that they were the ultimate targets of efforts to relax the previous norm of non-interference in internal affairs in order to complete the Western hegemonic project. This encouraged them to uphold the norm with greater conviction. Western governments would therefore be taking risks in wider political relations by commenting actively on events in Chechnya or human rights in China.

The distinction between defensive and offensive wars fits in with the distinction between wars of necessity and wars of choice.[14] Wars of necessity are prompted by direct threats to the survival of the state. With wars of choice there is no direct threat to primary interests: secondary interests may be at stake but the state will survive if no action is taken. In this context, the wars of necessity involve the defence of liberal values and those of choice involve their promotion. Wars of necessity are likely to be prompted by the rise of strong states – great powers – with the capacity to challenge the status quo. They are also likely to be fought between regular forces. Wars of choice, however, tend to reflect the problems of weak states and tend to involve irregular forces. Casualties in a war of necessity, to protect core values, to spare one's homeland from devastation or occupation by an alien power, might be unavoidable; casualties for more marginal political purposes, especially if these appear impossible to achieve, are much harder to justify.

Because Western liberal societies recoil at the inherent characteristics of war, they have recoiled at war itself, but when war is unavoidable they have sought to adapt it to render it more rational and controllable. The tension between waging wars for avowedly liberal ends but not always with evidently liberal means may be easier to manage in the case of defensive wars than offensive. Operations undertaken with the expressed aim of promoting liberal values but conducted with scant respect for individual life or dignity are likely to be futile and counter-productive in their consequences. In recent years there has been optimism about the developing possibilities for discrimination and precision in the application of force, thus making it possible to keep casualties on both sides down to the minimum and mitigating, if not eliminating, the most illiberal aspects of war. This helps to explain the tendency to seize on new technologies, as a means of turning war against its own nature.

The management of this tension between liberal ends and illiberal means is at the heart of many of the problems of contemporary strategy. All strategy is concerned with the relationship between ends and means, but military strategy is also about the relationship between two or more opposing forces. The ability to contain the effects of war depends not only on one's own strategic choices but also those of the opposing side. To the extent that attempts are being made to design strategies appropriate to liberal values, it may suit opponents to design strategies that thwart such attempts. For this reason, one of the core dilemmas identified by Western strategists is the tendency for asymmetry, whereby an attempt by one side to keep the fight focused on combatants and to spare civil society from damage, that is to render wars as regular as possible, might be countered by an opponent determined to push the conflict into civil society.

By the start of the twenty-first century, it seemed that it was only with some difficulty that Western states were edging towards a grand strategy appropriate for the new conditions. While events had cast them in the role of radicals, able to use their military and economic power to promote their ideology and change the behaviour of states reluctant to accept the values and practices of liberal capitalism, in other respects they were still conservative in nature. They hoped that the logic of the new situation would encourage others to embrace their values (which is what did happen in much of post-communist Europe), but when this did not happen their enthusiasm for radical initiatives was contained. It was hard to present the challenge ahead as a single campaign, into which a variety of types of activity might be integrated. Instead, particular events presented themselves as individual crises to which responses were often ad hoc, without an obvious pattern. Sometimes, therefore, governments were prepared to commit resources, to ask for sacrifices, to address public misgivings and to form international coalitions; sometimes they were not.

Rather than a coherent grand strategy specifying the role for armed force, the tendency instead was to produce tests that allowed the various relevant principles to be weighed against each other in the light of the features of a particular case. Two sets illustrate the possibilities of this approach. The first is connected with a cautious approach to interventions in third world conflicts and the second a more activist. After the 1982–4 debacle in Beirut, US Secretary of Defense Caspar Weinberger set down restrictive criteria for assessing future proposals for military interventions. The first test was that the US 'should not commit forces to combat over-seas unless the particular engagement or occasion is deemed vital to our national interest or that of our allies'. The other tests referred to the need, once a commitment had been made:

> to do so wholeheartedly and with the clear intention of winning, with clearly defined political and military objectives, continu-ally reassessing the relationship between our objectives and the forces committed, with the support of the American people and their elected representatives in Congress, and as a last resort.[15]

The logic of this position was that armed forces should be kept for the big occasions and that their use would be inappropriate when national interests were not at stake. There were two large political assumptions behind Weinberger's analysis. The first was dependence on the continuing support of public opinion, which in turn was dependent upon avoiding wars that were apt to become protracted, complex, indecisive and costly in casualties, without serving any vital interest. The second was that such wars were possible to avoid by focusing on aggressive states challenging the status quo while staying clear of conflicts underway within states.

By way of contrast, in a much-publicised speech in Chicago in April 1999, at a delicate period in the Kosovo campaign, British Prime Minister Tony Blair pondered the 'circumstances in which we should get actively involved in other peoples' conflicts'. At the time the British had framed defence policy in terms of an essentially altruistic foreign policy. The British *Strategic Defence Review* of 1998, for example, spoke of the military as a 'force for good'.[16] In his speech, Blair argued, on the one hand, for the need to qualify the principle of non-interference in the affairs of other states in the face of acts of genocide and oppression and when regimes are so narrowly based as to lack legitimacy. Yet, on the other, he accepted that it would be impossible to take on all undemocratic regimes engaged in acts of barbarity. He therefore suggested five tests as justification for intervention: a sure case; the exhaustion of all diplomatic options; the feasibility of sensible and prudent military operations; preparedness for a long-term commitment; and the involvement of some national interests.[17] The big difference was in the readiness even to contemplate interventions on matters in which the most vital interests were not engaged. After that, Blair's criteria were not notably more permissive than Weinberger's.

The 'global war on terror'

It was only with the terrorist attacks on the United States of 11 September 2001 that a unifying theme for Western grand strategy emerged. These attacks now appear as a turning point in international affairs as significant as the end of the Second World War in 1945 and the Cold War in 1989. They marked the end of the more optimistic years of the 1990s and set in motion a series of events that has transformed the foreign policy of the United States. From the start, President George W. Bush insisted that his country was at war. While the militants of al-Qaeda and its associates were described as challenging all civilised nations, the audacity and tragedy of the strikes against the Pentagon and the World Trade Center underscored the view that the United States was facing a unique threat and entitled to respond accordingly.

At the time of writing, this campaign can be said to have succeeded in one fundamental sense. Despite rumours and alarms, thus far there have been no further terrorist attacks of any size on American soil. Occasional, often quite deadly, attacks have taken place against allied and friendly countries although in no case have the militants been able to turn these into a state-threatening campaign (with the somewhat ironic exception of Iraq). The continuing sense of emergency, both nationally and internationally, including constant precautionary checks on people as they go about their daily business, and a reluctance to allow those who might be aiding, abetting, plotting or conducting acts of terror the normal protections of the law, has led to a presumption of apparently indefinite insecurity and accusations that this is being fostered for unconnected political, generally repressive purposes. The botched occupation of Iraq has made its own contribution, as has the damage done to both alliance relations and confidence in multilateral organisations. These are bad-tempered times.

From the start, the designation 'global war on terror' created anxiety among those who saw this as encouraging tendencies towards a militarised foreign policy or even a militarised society. A more benign explanation was that this was a war only as a rhetorical device along the lines of other wars, also proclaimed by presidents, against poverty, cancer or drugs. The best argument that 'war' is a wholly appropriate description of the struggle in which the United States is engaged is that its opponents also claim that they are engaged in a war. These claims had been made throughout the 1990s. There are good reasons to deny such groups the dignity of full-blooded enemy status. At some point, however, they become hard to dismiss as little more than a nuisance, as bands of fantasists and mischief-makers without significant support, and require extraordinary measures to prevent them from inflicting real harm. In this respect, the war did not start on 11 September 2001 but had begun, at least in jihadist eyes, much earlier. The jihadists believed themselves to be responding to a series of events, many of which had long faded from Western memories and were at any rate perceived as being quite disconnected, but which, to them, came together as part of a generalised Western war against Islam. Moreover, the jihadists had already mounted a number of attacks, with varying degrees of success, against American targets. The significance of the declaration of war by the US government was that it could no longer deny the existence of a struggle that was already underway.

But with whom were the Americans struggling? A general 'war on terror' lacks political context. Terrorism may be a state of mind but it is not a state, nor even a political movement. The use of terror, especially when it takes the form of random, vicious attacks against defenceless and innocent civilians, may reveal many of a group's values and ultimate objectives but it is still essentially a tactic and might be discarded for other tactics without the group itself believing much has changed. The tactic is one traditionally favoured by insurgents and insurrectionists because they lack the direct means of challenging the armed forces of the state. By itself it is normally a poor tactic as it has rarely served by itself to mobilise popular support against the state, and when that popular support already exists then alternative methods to terrorism are often possible. Because the term is pejorative, normally used to smear opponents, few groups actually proclaim themselves to be terrorists. To understand those who do resort to terroristic tactics it is helpful to consider their ideology and political programme as a whole. It then becomes apparent that many quite distinctive groups have indulged in terrorism, which is why analysts tend to distinguish between religious, nationalist, leftist, rightist and cultist types. In principle, therefore, a war on terror can take in campaigns against a large range of groups with very little else in common beyond their chosen tactics. At one point, the White House mooted 'Struggle Against Violent Extremism' (SAVE) as a preferable slogan to the 'Global War on Terror', but this never really caught on, and the president found that it lacked the immediate impact of the slogan that had first come to mind. If SAVE had been adopted this would potentially have broadened the campaign even more and brought no new clarity to the situation. The references in the 2006 QDR to the 'long war' say something sobering about duration though nothing about content.

In this respect, one objective could be to establish a new norm of inter-national politics, to the effect that terrorist methods are illegitimate in all circumstances, so almost any cause might be invalidated by their adoption. This could follow the attempt to create a norm of humanitarian interven-tion. Indeed there are important links between the acts which prompt humanitarian intervention and those which prompt a war on terrorism. In both cases the victims are most likely to be defenceless civilians. The moral objection lies in the use of violent means against non-combatants for political objectives. In both cases, taking action is likely to mean ignoring inhibitions against interfering in the internal affairs of other states.

In another sense, however, there is an important difference. Vicious domestic persecution or ethnic cleansing are weapons used by the strong against the weak, so that the weak can only find redress if those who are attacking them are in turn attacked by even stronger powers, which is why this becomes a test for a contemporary form of internationalism. Terrorism, by contrast, is a weapon habitually used by the weak against the strong. It is a form of response that does not rely on taking on the enemy at its stron-gest point but instead looking for vulnerabilities in its social structure. So while the victims of ethnic cleansing and other human rights abuses have by definition already been marginalised, the victims of terrorism are more likely to be found in the cities of the strong. This is why it is more likely to prompt a response by the strong and why a war to ease humanitar-ian distress may well be against the established regime, yet a war against terrorism may well be in its support.

There is evidence that revulsion at a particular sort of political violence as used by one group delegitimises it for others and that can have impor-tant political consequences. For example, the Provisional Irish Republican Army soon realised in late 2001 that the American people were going to be less inclined to see the romance in their 'military operations' against the British state and more likely to see the menace. At the same time, the origins and character of political violence can be so various that blanket denunciations may soon lead to awkward associations with states using subtler or at least more covert forms of oppression, or fine judgements in situations where many groups are engaged in violence against each other, all claiming it to be for self-defence.

The alternative is to accept that the war is with a political group, but here different problems arise because there are no single words to describe a complex phenomenon. All descriptions are loaded. It is clearly much more than al-Qaeda, because that label does not speak for all the relevant jihadist activists and is now a rather capacious umbrella under which many groups find cover. To agree that this is a global struggle linking many conflicts across many regions, all involving Muslim populations but otherwise quite disparate, is to concede a lot. From the Western perspective, Kashmir, Afghanistan, Indonesia, Iraq, Palestine, Chechnya, Uzbekistan, Bosnia and Kosovo, and many more countries, all seem to be quite different in many respects, including in their impact on Western sympathies. If they are all of a piece for many activists who travel from one to the other on the assumption that they are moving to different fronts of the same war, then the strategic challenge may be to undermine rather than to reinforce that assumption. The fact that they act in the name of Islam does not mean that a certain sort of austere literalism in belief and behaviour leads inexorably to approval for violence against civilian unbelievers or apostates. Furthermore, this highly politicised version of Islam with quasi-clerical leadership is challenged by those who believe that the clergy should confine themselves to spiritual matters. In general, the terms 'jihadist', which has a more warrior-like connotation (although 'jihad' can be used in a moderate form and not necessarily just as 'holy war' involving armed struggle), and al-Qaeda, accepting that this includes a number of loosely affiliated groups, are used here.

The philosophy animating these groups contains common elements. They see Western countries as threatening both because of the values they represent (secular and liberal) and their past role in supporting oppressive and corrupt regimes. Their long-term objectives are to re-establish the old caliphate and to insist on the full application of sharia law. More immediately, their aim is to persuade Western states to disengage from conflicts and countries involving Muslim populations and to desist from supporting regimes which crack down on popular Islamic movements. There are, in addition, often more apocalyptical notions swirling around the writings and speeches of the leaders of these groups, claiming vengeance for past wrongs and offering uncompromising visions of the struggle. These groups are profoundly illiberal in their instinct for theocracy, their intolerance of diversity and dissent, and their homophobia and misogyny. Yet at the same time they can play on themes which liberals recognise, including anti-imperialism and the sense of outrage and grievance among the poor and dispossessed, as well as distaste for many of the regimes which the West has backed in the past, and in some cases still backs.

Whether or not the terminology is appropriate, the 'global war on terror' has undoubtedly brought to a head all the tensions inherent in a liberal grand strategy. The enemy poses a direct challenge to liberal values, in terms of both narrow and broad definitions, and is by the same token vulnerable to the spread of these values. Jihadism is unlikely to prosper in functioning liberal democracies and efficient market economies. Yet, in other respects, it is a product of globalisation. The underlying vision is internationalist, with little respect for state boundaries. It is able to take full advantage of modern forms of communication and the ease with which money can be moved. In this regard, there is often an overlap with criminal organisations, which take advantage of the same facilities. It therefore adds to the pressure to monitor and regulate these facilities. In addition, many of the regimes fighting terrorism are illiberal and even liberal regimes have made cases for illiberal measures, albeit on an emergency basis.

President Bush framed the response to 9/11 in terms of national security and it was on this basis that Afghanistan and Iraq were occupied. Within this framework it was accepted that the insidious nature of the threat required measures that could not be guaranteed to accord at all times with liberal values. In light of its experience since 2003 the Bush administration might wish it had handled matters differently. In particular, this experience has pointed to the perils of ignoring questions of legitimacy in the conduct of military operations.

CHAPTER THREE

Asymmetric War

The 2006 QDR discusses the special challenges posed by terrorist networks in the context of the wider problem of asymmetric threats. This problem is a natural consequence of US superiority in conventional capabilities. In the past, in conflicts between advanced states it was presumed that while variations between individual weapons types might make a difference, there would be broad symmetries between the belligerents, thus placing an even greater premium on numbers, training and tactics. In practice, the United States has pulled ahead technologically from even its closest allies and certainly its old enemies. It now accounts for half of all world military expenditure and other Western countries for about another third. It has prepared itself for a game that only it can play in a league in which it is the sole participant. Even if China were to challenge the United States, the most likely trigger for a major clash of this sort would be Taiwan and that would be, at least in the first instance, as much a naval as a land battle. It is hard to imagine contingencies in which the United States would seek to defeat the army of another major power, or indeed circumstances in which another major power would knowingly try to defeat the United States in conventional battle. This does not mean that future inter-state wars are impossible, with or without the United States, or that they might not take on the form of classical conventional warfare. It does, nonetheless, put a large question mark against the notion of a true revolution in military affairs because of the unlikelihood that all serious powers as well as aspirants will structure their armed forces in similar ways to prepare for some rather standardised encounters.

The issue is not simply one of a basic power imbalance. The strategic choices apparently mandated by the RMA do not so much slavishly follow a line of technological development, but rather a line of political expectation and of ethical thinking in Western societies, based on the Christian just war tradition and liberal values, with questions of discrimination and proportionality in warfare to the fore.[1] It assumes the following elements:

- Professionalism of armed forces. High-quality weaponry reduces the relative importance of numbers, although it also puts a premium on high-quality troops.
- Decisive force directed to clear political ends. The military expect to be set well-defined objectives by their political masters, which it is their job to meet, preferably without further political interference.
- Intolerance of casualties. Even with professional forces there is an expectation that strategies should be designed to keep casualties to a minimum.
- Intolerance of collateral damage. If war is the responsibility of governments and armed forces but not the population at large then all civilians must be deemed innocent unless proven guilty. This argues for targeting military assets rather than people.

There is, therefore, a connecting theme of separating the military from the civil, of combatants from non-combatants, of fire from society, of organised violence from everyday life. So long as armed forces are organised around the belief in victory through decisive battle, this should be achieved as quickly and as painlessly as possible, with the minimum of damage to civilian life and property. For a war to be fought along these lines not only must the belligerents have acquired comparable substantial and advanced military capabilities but they must also inhabit the same moral and political universe.

If they do, of course, then the narrative surrounding the conflict can be confusing. By and large it is politically convenient to be able to portray enemies as inhabiting a quite different and invariably disagreeable moral universe that provides them with rationalisations for terrible deeds. It thus helped the British government in the 1982 Falklands War that it was facing a military junta, just as it helped in 1991 that Saddam Hussein was an established mass-murderer and serial aggressor. So an enemy committed to fighting on Western terms would be problematic in its own way. One that spared civil society, minimalised casualties all round, allowed civilians their sanctuaries, honoured the Geneva Conventions and generally targeted systems rather than people would not suggest a propensity for barbarism. However, enemies that prefer to use brains rather than brawn and do not want to cause too much hurt are not only hard to find but might also be expected to be prepared to resolve differences without resort to arms. The vast literature on the circumstances in which democracies go to war makes it clear that at the very least it is more likely against enemies whose political structures and methods are objectionable from the start.

At any rate, given that it is now even harder to find enemies who are capable of fighting on Western terms even if they wanted to, those that actually do exist will adopt strategies that give them a fighting chance, even though they are unconventional and deeply unpleasant. Until quite recently, the members of NATO were, at least in principle, prepared to threaten nuclear attacks to deter aggression. The risk of having to implement that threat was extremely small, though large enough to have the requisite deterrent effect, but the fact remains that reliance upon the most complete of all threats to civil society was until very recently a centrepiece of Western strategy. It was not because of an increased moral maturity that nuclear deterrence ceased to be the centrepiece of western strategy for dealing with conventional threats but because it was possible to deal effectively with such threats on their own terms, without escalation. The incentives for escalation now lie with the adversaries.

The obvious point, found in much of the commentary on the RMA, is that those who are almost bound to lose wars fought on Western terms have every incentive to adopt alternative strategies that play to their advantages. These could be found in geography (short supply lines and opportunities for urban warfare), a threshold of pain (a readiness to accept casualties), patience (leading to frustration in Western capitals) and even a relative lack of humanitarian scruples (allowing the war to extend into civil society). These are now described as asymmetric strategies. If the promise of precision warfare lies in keeping casualties and economic damage down on both sides and confining them largely to the military sphere, the same logic might lead those seeking to discourage Western military action to adopt tactics and weapons that have exactly the opposite effects. While precision warfare allows for strategies designed to limit the damage on all sides, it does not preclude strategies based on alternative assumptions. New options are also emerging for those anxious to maximise the human cost of war. Though there may be less excuse for crude and indiscriminate modes of war-fighting with the systems associated with the RMA, they do provide opportunities for those who deliberately seek to target civil society. One side may boast that the accuracy of its weapons allows it to avoid nuclear power plants, hospitals and apartment blocks. Another may be pleased to use the same accuracy to score direct hits on these targets so as to maximise rather than minimise human suffering.

In addition, the technological breakthroughs of the middle of the last century, represented by nuclear weapons and long-range missiles, are still with us. They expanded the means of destruction and extended the range through which they could be applied. Attempts to mitigate their effects, for example through improving anti-missile defences, have been far less impressive. The capability to destroy hundreds of thousands of human beings in a nuclear flash therefore remains part of our everyday reality and, despite the cumulative efforts of the abolitionists, is likely to be so for the foreseeable future.[2] Chemical weapons first made their presence felt during the First World War. There may, of course, be other technologies that are still in their infancy but which might have startling effects. The biotechnologies, for example, have so far been less conspicuous in their conventional military applications than electronics. They appear more in predictions of grotesque and malign types of weapons.[3] If the main business of warfare is to eliminate or paralyse the opponent's military capacity then these forms of destruction appear as unnecessarily cruel and ruinous. But if the main business is to intimidate, to coerce, or simply to wreak vengeance then it makes a sort of sense to target civil society. Just as NATO was prepared to adopt policies of nuclear deterrence when it felt conventionally inferior, when the old balance of conventional power was reversed Russia adopted a similar posture.

The idea of asymmetric conflict has been around since the 1970s, as a reflection of the Vietnam experience.[4] The first explicit mention of the concept in a Pentagon document was in the 1995 *Joint Doctrine*,[5] in a reference to engagements between dissimilar forces. In this context asymmetry could work to the advantage of the US in line with its comparative advantages. Thus USAF General Ronald R. Fogelman spoke in 1996 of a 'new American way of war':

> America has not only the opportunity but the obligation to transition from a concept of annihilation and attrition warfare that places thousands of young Americans at risk in brute, force-on-force conflicts to a concept that leverages our sophisticated military capabilities to achieve US objectives by applying what I like to refer to as an 'asymmetric force' strategy.[6]

As it became apparent that it would suit the US to fight symmetrically, on its terms, asymmetry acquired more negative implications. The 1997 QDR observed that: 'US dominance in the conventional military arena may encourage adversaries to use ... asymmetric means to attack our interests overseas and Americans at home'.[7] The basic frustration with this approach was summed up in a 1998 report from the National Defense University which characterised asymmetry as not 'fighting fair'.[8] As the concept moved into the wider policy debate, the inclination was to develop a generic concept. Thus the 1999 *Joint Strategy Review*[9] defined asymmetric approaches as those that attempted 'to circumvent or undermine US strengths while exploiting US weaknesses using methods that differ significantly from the United States' expected method of operations'. These could be applied 'at all levels of warfare – strategic, operational, land tactical – and across the spectrum of military operations'. Put this way the approach becomes synonymous with any sound strategy for fighting the United States and loses any specificity. Moreover, this generic depiction of asymmetric warfare encourages the analysis to start with an appreciation of US vulnerabilities which is likely to reflect the concerns of the moment (information warfare against critical infrastructure, weapons of mass destruction) rather than the opponent's mind-set. Thus the critical planning document released in 2000, *Joint Vision 2020*, unlike its 1995 predecessor, *Joint Vision 2010*,[10] did address the problem, but used as a key example the threat of long-range ballistic missiles. This, of course, was against the background policy debate of the moment, which was whether the United States should opt to develop a new missile-defence system.

At the end of September 2001, as Washington was still mulling over how best to deal with al-Qaeda, the Pentagon published its new QDR, which included a reference to the necessity to 'degrade an aggressor's ability to coerce others through conventional or asymmetric means, including CBRNE [chemical, biological, radiological, nuclear and enhanced high explosive] weapons'. So while references to asymmetric warfare were plentiful, the concept was still largely linked to proper war, serving as an argument for missile defences. It was not linked to 'small-scale contingencies' which would best be undertaken in concert with allies and friends and by specialised units.[11] Even studies which, after 11 September 2001, could claim to have been prescient in their warnings about the hazards of 'super-terrorism', tended to discourage a focus on al-Qaeda. Thus the Hart–Rudman Commission, which had identified 'unannounced attacks on American cities' as the gravest threat, also suggested that 'terrorism will appeal to many weak states as an attractive, asymmetric option to blunt the influence of major powers. Hence, state-sponsored terrorist attacks are at least as likely, if not more so, than attacks by independent, unaffiliated terrorist groups.'[12] North Korea and Iraq once again appeared as likely culprits, so that this threat also could be seen as having its most credible form in a derivative of the standard scenarios. In the 2006 QDR the asymmetric problem is taken to refer to both irregular warfare and WMD.

In retrospect, the notion of asymmetric war turned out to be less helpful than at first assumed. To observe that an enemy unable to fight on one's own terms is likely to fight differently is banal. Listing the potential sources of difference can involve mentioning all aspects of warfare, including political factors such as motivation and alliances, or geographical factors, such as familiarity with terrain and occupation of high ground, as well as capabilities and strategic preferences. A more serious problem was that a reference to asymmetric warfare turned into a strong proposition that the natural incentive for those facing the conventional superiority of the United States and its allies was to opt for WMD as the natural means of playing on the West's preference for more people-friendly forms of warfare. The shock of 9/11 reinforced this view, encouraging a focus on a particularly dire scenario in which terrorist groups had possession of the most deadly weapons. The United States had taken on board the notion of asymmetric war but had geared it to the dominant scenarios guiding all American force planning. These still pointed to proper wars between the armed forces of major powers, with far less attention being given to those lesser, irregular types.

Irregular warfare

Up to this point the problem of irregular warfare had come to be associated with humanitarian interventions. The key feature of these interventions was that they sought to influence the character and course of a developing conflict which was neither taking place upon nor directly threatening national territory and did not relate to any specific obligations to allies. Thus they involved intervention in conflicts that were already underway and lacked any overriding strategic imperative. Beyond that, this category encompassed a wide range of possibilities. The conflict could be developing within one particular state or involve a number of states; its stage of development could be early or quite mature; and it could range from sporadic skirmishing to significant battles. Interventions could take a range of forms: from enforcing a blockade to clearing the skies of aircraft engaged in prohibited activities; from providing humanitarian relief to taking and defending territory. They also had an unavoidably discretionary aspect. At any given time there were numerous conflicts underway, many of a long-standing and murderous consistency. It would simply be beyond the capacity of willing interveners and international organisations to deal with all but a few of these at any given time.

The United States had not been a willing intervener. This was because of three aspects of these sorts of interventions which were likely to make them unpopular with the military and with the public: the tendency of 'mission creep'; the likelihood of casualties when no vital interests were at stake; and the distraction from preparations for proper war.

Mission creep

Military officers yearn for a precise definition of aim against which they can plan and judge success, and that, crucially, tells them when they and their troops are allowed to go home. Yet interventions in civil wars were unlikely to have clear-cut, let alone happy, endings. 'Mission creep' entered the strategic lexicon during the 1990s to describe the irritating tendency of interventions to move out of whatever boundaries had been originally set for them. One reason for this was the tendency to set forces at a level proportionate to the interests at stake. This could lead to token contributions, which was likely to lead to futility. It is as difficult to intervene marginally as it is to be slightly pregnant. The mere act of using military force symbolises resolve and deep concern and so can convey determination. However, symbols without substance, for example deployments well away from the area of any likely hostilities and with extremely restricted rules of engagement, are most likely to convey a lack of resolve. It may be true in international politics as in plays, as Chekhov once observed, that if a gun appears on the wall in Act One you can be sure that it will have been used by Act Three. Governments might agree to operations with quite limited liabilities, but once engagement has begun, and little is being achieved, then there will be pressure to increase force contributions and activity levels. Disengagement involves severe reputational risks. The internal dynamics of these conflicts can shift alarmingly, often to the point that common decency requires additional effort by outside forces to prevent some calamity. If force levels and tactics are set solely in relation to the interests at stake they may have little relation to those of the opponents: limited means are not necessarily sufficient to support limited interests. Extra forces, however, do not guarantee speedy solutions. Because their origins lie in inter-communal conflict these interventions are hard to bring to an end. In addition, the military find that civilian agencies assume that they have infinite resources to solve problems well beyond their traditional role, from feeding refugees to basic police duties.

It was Bosnia that encouraged the notion of 'mission creep', as UN troops with a peacekeeping mandate were told to protect Muslim safe areas from Serb aggression without being properly prepared for this new task. If they took their role seriously then they were at severe risk; if they failed to do so, then tragedy and disillusion could result. Richard Cheney (as a former secretary of defense) observed in 1993:

> I don't think that advocates of U.S. military force to end the bloodshed in Bosnia have properly considered what would be entailed … You need an objective that you can define in military terms … If you say, 'Go in and stop the bloodshed in Bosnia,' that's not sufficiently clear to build a mission around. Does that mean you're going to put a U.S. soldier between every Bosnian Serb and Bosnian Muslim? You also need to know what constitutes victory. How would you define it? How would you know when you achieved it?[13]

Richard Holbrooke, the American negotiator of the Dayton accords, later complained in his book *To End a War*, that the military used 'mission creep' as 'a powerful pejorative'. It conjured up 'images of quagmire', he noted, without ever being clearly defined. It was always used in a negative sense to kill a proposal.[14]

The military's desire for a clear task it can execute according to its best professional judgement is understandable. In serious combat with enemy armed forces they expect to be spared from constant political interference once the basic rules of engagement have been set. It is also the case that forces becoming involved in civil wars are unlikely to have a simple straightforward mission. External intervention normally involves a number of inter-weaving civilian and military strands and disparate national and international agencies in conditions which can change quite rapidly. But in these complex civil–military conflicts the military's role is always likely to evolve. Whether the mission is to contain the conflict, to set rules for its conduct, to ease suffering or to broker a settlement, there is bound to be a dynamic interaction with the interests of the local parties. Thus intervention has to be recognised not as being directed against a specific end, but as being part of a process, though undoubtedly a process with defined stages. Military action alone can never be sufficient: at best it can create conditions for a more favourable political outcome. Only once the fragility of local institutions, infrastructure and economic activity is addressed will it be safe to leave. By definition, a country which can only be stabilised by outside intervention is no longer fully self-governing.

The very fact that military measures have had to be employed means that some parties whose consent may be essential to the viability of a political solution feel bitter and cheated. By the time military action has become necessary it must be assumed that satisfactory solutions based on harmony, justice and consensus are no longer possible, at least not in the short term. The uncertain political support for these operations, especially after the Somalia debacle, led the Americans to insist on an 'exit strategy' even as they entered a conflict. In Bosnia a firm timetable (geared to the 1996 presidential election in the US) had to be abandoned as it became apparent that early withdrawal would result in instability. Insisting on an 'exit strategy' at the point of entry was something of a giveaway, encouraging the opponent to threaten an interminable conflict, in which the fighting would be long term and bitter, even if also spasmodic and at a low level.

Casualty aversion

Since the later stages of the Vietnam War it has been taken for granted that there is low popular tolerance for high casualty rates in any conflict falling short of an existential struggle for national survival. Some were prepared to see this as a secular trend, the consequences of a post-heroic age,[15] although past ages were not always that heroic, except in an involuntary sense. There was a presumption that there would be increasing reluctance to put the young generation at risk in war, even with all-volunteer forces. Yet, in the 1991 Gulf War, Western countries were prepared to accept substantial casualties in order to reverse aggression. Few anticipated the modest scale of casualties resulting directly from *Desert Storm*. Equally, and in part because of this, few anticipated the heavy casualties, over time, suffered in the 2003 Iraq War, which resulted in a build-up of political opposition clearly linked to the lack of commensurate political gain. In his work on Vietnam, John Mueller argued that there was a direct link between support for the war and the level of casualties.[16] Later work has questioned the suggested automaticity of more casualties and less support. In Vietnam, the key was the growing sense of the pointlessness of the sacrifice and its lack of proportion to the real interests at stake in the conflict. More recent analysis has stressed the relevance of the objective of the military mission and the resulting success or failure. This means that support for intervening in civil wars is low, multilateral support matters and that there is a preference for less risky options such as air strikes.[17] A study carried out in 1999 by the Triangle Institute of Security Studies, which demonstrated that even in a case where it would be assumed that casualty tolerance would be close to zero (action to stabilise a democratic government in the Congo), the public was not only prepared to accept quite high levels of combat deaths, but that these levels were significantly higher than those accepted by the civilian elite, and even more so than the military elite. This led to the bizarre conclusion (pre-Iraq) that senior military officers had become more casualty averse than the average American citizen.[18] The notion of casualty intolerance had become so internalised that military and political leaders had become loath to put it to the test.

The strength of the presumption of casualty intolerance was illustrated in the US Army's 1993 *Field Manual 100-5: Operations*. 'The American people expect decisive victory and abhor unnecessary casualties. They prefer quick resolution of conflicts and reserve the right to reconsider their support should any of these conditions not be met.'[19] This led to what Jeffrey Record described as 'Force-Protection Fetishism'. The result of this fetish was that lack of loss – not mission accomplishment – becomes the standard for judging an operational success.[20] The 1999 Kosovo War demonstrated the impact of this concern and, despite the consequences it had for mission accomplishment in terms of relieving the developing humanitarian catastrophe, it was considered to have been validated. When Secretary of Defense William S. Cohen and Chairman of the Joint Chiefs of Staff General Henry H. Shelton identified the 'paramount lesson learned from Operation Allied Force' it was that 'the wellbeing of our people must remain our first priority'.[21] As a US Army brigade moved into Kosovo as part of the force intended to bring some calm to the country after the war, its mission statement listed as its first priority 'self-protection' with the 'peacekeeping tasks' secondary. US troops stayed, separated from the society which they were supposed to help calm, in a guarded and well-appointed compound, while the troops of allies intermingled with the local population.

When the risk of the combination of casualties and futility appears high, governments have been quick to extricate themselves. The withdrawals in response to the 241 marines lost in the October 1983 attack on their barracks in Beirut and the loss of 18 rangers in Somalia a decade later suggested that there were some causes that were not worth a substantial loss of life. This was despite explanations for withdrawal other than the absolute level of casualties. Notably, most European countries have been less affected by casualty aversion than the United States. France took casualties in Lebanon and Bosnia regularly without evidently flinching, while Britain, with years of steady losses in Northern Ireland, made the case for taking the risk of a ground offensive in Kosovo. The idea that casualty intolerance was a particularly American vulnerability had strategic consequences and gave ideas to the opponents of the United States. Osama bin Laden, for example, in an interview prior to 9/11 made specific mention of the rush to get out of Somalia. He remarked on how his comrades who had fought in Somalia had been surprised by the 'low spiritual morale' of the Americans. He noted how 'the largest power on earth' left 'after some resistance from powerless, poor, unarmed people'.[22]

Lesser contingencies

Humanitarian interventions were also resented as a distraction from the main business of preparing for a major war. This assumed, as the 1997 National Defense Panel put it, that the relatively calm, international environment of the 1990s was no more than an 'interlude'. Eventually a serious 'peer competitor' would emerge, ready to challenge the benign hegemony of the United States. The penalties could be severe if investment for this moment was neglected because of a distracting preoccupation with 'recent trends in civil disturbance',[23] leading to a chase after minor irritants.

Colin Powell, who rose to high office working closely with Weinberger under President Ronald Reagan and then became chairman of the Joint Chiefs of Staff under George H.W. Bush and Bill Clinton, was very much of the view that American military power was best employed in an overwhelming manner to achieve clearly defined objectives with both speed and minimum casualties.[24] He was particularly dismissive of the idea of using American forces on such inappropriate tasks as 'constabulary duties'.[25] Out of this came the critical distinction between real 'war', defined in terms of 'large-scale combat operations', and 'operations other than war', which included shows of force, operations for the purposes of peace enforcement and peacekeeping, and counter-terrorism and counter-insurgency. These latter types of operations were much more discretionary and, it was clearly implied, best avoided.[26] The sort of improper war the military had in mind was the earlier stages of the Vietnam War which had been conducted as a counter-insurgency campaign against Viet Cong guerrillas. So while the military expected few political restraints on how they might go about war-fighting they sought to establish restraints on the wars that should be fought.[27] The US military establishment became so reluctant to engage in small wars that it failed to prepare for them.[28] By 1986, even *Field Manual 90-8: Counterguerrilla Operations*, dealing with action directed against armed anti-government forces, was claiming that the 'basic concept of AirLand Battle doctrine can be applied to Counterguerrilla operations'.[29]

Throughout the 1990s, the US military remained wary of irregular wars and refused to make major changes in doctrine and training to accommodate them, insisting that forces optimised for large-scale conventional war would be able to accomplish other, supposedly less demanding, tasks. General Wesley K. Clark's account of the management of the Kosovo War, from his vantage point as Supreme Allied Commander Europe, makes clear that – as far as the Pentagon was concerned – the demands of this campaign should not be allowed to reduce preparedness for the planning priorities of Iraq and North Korea.[30] *Joint Vision 2010* sought to build on the country's 'core strengths of high quality people and information-age technological advances' by developing four operational concepts: 'dominant maneuver, precision engagement, full dimensional protection, and focused logistics'. It claimed that the application of these concepts would provide 'Full Spectrum Dominance', a capability 'to dominate an opponent across the range of military operations'.[31] Priority was nonetheless given to preparations for major war, on the off-chance that there might be a very large-scale contingency at some point in the future, effectively dismissing the relatively small-scale contingencies that became common in the 1990s as secondary and residual.[32] Once they were viewed as 'lesser-included cases', the special demands, in terms of equipment mixes, training and rules of engagement, made by these smaller-scale contingencies, were not accorded the same priority as the major contingencies.[33]

All these factors influenced the incoming Bush administration in 2001, which was therefore expected to share this reluctance to address lesser contingencies. The prospective national security advisor, Condoleezza Rice, observed that:

> The president must remember that the military is a special instrument. It is lethal, and it is meant to be. It is not a civilian peace force. It is not a political referee. And it is most certainly not designed to build a civilian society. Military force is best used to support clear political goals, whether limited, such as expelling Saddam from Kuwait, or comprehensive, such as demanding the unconditional surrender of Japan and Germany during World War II.

From this she drew the conclusions that US intervention in 'humanitarian' crises would be at best 'exceedingly rare'. The criteria for becoming involved were familiar: the president should ask 'whether decisive force is possible and is likely to be effective and must know how and when to get out'. Humanitarian interventions were thus largely jobs for allies.[34]

CHAPTER FOUR

The Transformation of Military Strategy

During the 1990s, the United States adopted not only a concept of proper and largely regular war, for which it could develop a formidable strategy, but also a concept of improper and largely irregular wars, for which it could not. One response by its enemies might be to draw it into an irregular war on the ground. This could be avoided by staying clear of contingencies which were likely to involve irregular combat.

The temptation of air power

Proper war has had a clear operational sequence. This was followed meticulously in the 1991 Gulf War: first, remove the enemy air defences and then go for strategic targets. These ranged from the obviously military, including command and control bunkers, to the militarily relevant, for example energy and transport, and on to the more effectively civilian, such as the so-called 'leadership targets'. The next phase involved the preparation of the battlefield prior to the land battle, with the evident hope that strategic airpower would prove decisive before this point was reached. Since then, as a result of the growing air superiority of the US, these stages have been contracted. It is no longer necessary to spend so long on air defences. In the campaigns against Iraq in 1991 and Yugoslavia later in the decade, air defences were a serious issue as they were based on the equipment and systems adopted by Warsaw Pact countries. The Iraqi system in particular was extraordinarily extensive, built up as a result of the war with Iran and the Israeli attack on the Osiraq nuclear reactor in 1981. Much of it was destroyed during the first weeks of the 1991 war. Attempts to reconstruct the defences were constantly thwarted during the various spats between the US and the Iraqis, resulting from the coalition's constant air patrols, so that by the 2003 war Iraq could do little.

It was clear from the 1991 Gulf War onwards that it was impossible to conduct a conventional ground war while having conceded command of the air. The allies could always fight in three dimensions while Iraq was confined to only two. Without air protection, a dug-in army is doomed over time, while one on the move is highly vulnerable as soon as it is spotted. Meanwhile, an offensive enjoying air superiority can move very quickly indeed. The advantage in land war was not with the defence or the offence but the side with air superiority. With air power, a modest margin of superiority in capability tends to translate into a decisive margin in battle. This was not the same, however, as arguing that it could be used strategically, independently of land forces and also without devastating enemy society. Regardless, the evident comparative advantage of the West in airpower means that it appears as a virtually risk-free military option. If air power were an area of undisputed superiority and land operations carried the risk of severe casualties then the optimum strategy would rely on air power alone. This option became extremely tempting when some involvement in improper wars became unavoidable, because it meant that US forces could keep clear of one of their most hazardous aspects, taking on irregular forces on the ground.

Air – or cruise missile – strikes were often invoked as the first tough measures to be taken after diplomatic isolation and economic sanctions were perceived to have failed. It is almost the military equivalent of break-ing diplomatic relations – something that is relatively painless for the instigator to do though it may not actually be very helpful. Air defences became targets of choice not because they were essential to securing air superiority but because they had notional military value and rarely involved casualties, and so might make some coercive point without causing a political storm. The claim that airpower could defeat a deter-mined enemy on its own depended on the 'centres of gravity' approach.[1] This involved a crude political theory, which worked on the assumptions that a society can be understood as a closed interdependent system in which damage to a few critical components can bring everything else to a grinding halt and also that this can be achieved from the air. It was always likely that attempts to break an enemy state through air raids would involve inflicting real pain on the enemy's society. The lesson from the old debate on strategic bombardment – that attacks on an enemy population cannot by themselves break the will of the enemy government – did not lead to the corollary that the fate of the enemy population is somehow irrelevant and that the government's standing can readily be broken by other means. Inevitably, and despite self-denying ordinances about attacking civilian targets, it was the targets that were relevant to both civilian and military affairs that were chosen. Some caused more hurt. Attacks on energy supplies might not cause too many casualties, but, as it was discovered after the 1991 Gulf War, the long-term effect on a society could be disastrous, especially if water supplies were harmed. The basic problem remained that very few political objectives could be met directly by air attack alone. Its use can influence the victim's calculations, but it cannot achieve the physical control of enemy decision-making that is always at least a theoretical possibility following a land offensive.

The idea that air power might work on its own, at least as a coercive instrument, gained support during the 1990s through a selective reading of the critical events. Slowly but surely during the Bosnian conflict, those involved, including NATO and the UN, realised that they were moving a long way from traditional peacekeeping involving collections of lightly armed, indifferently trained troops. At best, such forces alleviated local distress and diverted the fighting elsewhere; at worst they created a vulnerability that would argue against a more robust stand at a later date. There were still occasions when minimal force would be needed, but it had become apparent that external interventions designed to ease and overcome conflicts could require active and often robust military operations.[2] Establishing 'no-fly' zones, as was done over Bosnia as well as Iraq, could only have a limited effect on the main struggle for power going on below where there had been less success in establishing 'no-artillery' zones and 'no-ethnic cleansing' zones.

Demands for a more robust approach always pointed to an increased use of airpower. When this came in Bosnia, with *Operation Deliberate Force* in 1995,[3] preceding the Dayton settlement, this was considered a great success. It was described in 1997 'as the prime modern example of how judicious use of airpower, coupled with hard-nosed diplomacy, can stop a ground force in its tracks and bring the worst of enemies to the bargaining table'.[4] The basis of this claim is that, while it was underway, Ambassador Richard Holbrooke, then US Assistant Secretary of State for European and Canadian Affairs, was busy negotiating with the Bosnian Serb leadership on behalf of the contact group which led to the Dayton conference and eventually to a settlement.[5] Yet in *Deliberate Force* the bombing was not initiated to influence the peace process. It was represented officially as an effort to protect the safe areas and, in particular, Sarajevo. Nor was it graduated according to the requirements of diplomacy. It may have sapped the Serbs' will to fight but their basic problem was that the ground war had turned. The Croatian army had pushed Serbs out of western Slavonia and Krajina and within Bosnia the Serb hold on territory had dropped from 70% to about 50% as a result of Croat and Muslim offensives. In addition, the UN forces had moved into more defensive positions, while elements of NATO's rapid reaction force deployed into the Sarajevo area from mid-June shelled Serb forces at the start of the air campaign. From this experience, the West concluded correctly that diplomacy in the Balkans had to be backed by credible force, but, less reliably, that this could be provided through the severe but measured application of air power.

Led by President Bill Clinton, NATO decided that it could repeat this misinterpreted experience in 1999 in order to persuade the Serb leadership to call off its ethnic cleansing of Kosovo and to withdraw its forces. During the Kosovo air campaign, NATO was caught out by the unrealistic expectations it had perpetuated about avoiding collateral damage. Great attention was paid by the media to 'blunders'. Once exacting standards for precision are set, the routine tragedies of past wars can appear as outrages that threaten to invalidate the whole purpose of a modern war. As appropriate targets may well lie in the grey area between the strictly military and the civil, Western countries will inevitably fall short of these standards. Public opinion often appeared uncomfortable with the results of NATO's bombing but still recognised that terrible things happen in war by accident as well as by design and, critically, took the view that those who initiate violence should not be surprised if it comes to engulf their societies.

The air threat posed to Serbia and its armed forces up to late March 1999 was large enough to signal an interest but insufficient to compel the target to change its behaviour. It was reasonable for the Serbs to assume that they would have to face little more than four days of raids on air defence sites and command centres. Once its bluff was called, NATO had to implement this inadequate threat with initially inadequate results. The level of air strikes was raised in a hurry, increasing the risk not so much of casualties but of blunders and moving to what was by necessity in practice, a punitive campaign. The evidence of Kosovo suggests that it was the impact on the civilian sphere that made the most difference, as the quality of life in Serbia steadily deteriorated under the impact of NATO's air bombardment. Attempts to target Serb military capabilities, especially those engaged in ethnic cleansing, were hampered by the use of concealment, camouflage and dummy equipment. Increased Kosovo Liberation Army (KLA) activity made a difference, especially when this forced Serb units out into the open where they could be more readily targeted by NATO aircraft. The damage to the Serb economic – as much as military – infrastructure probably contributed to Belgrade's decision to agree to terms. The fact that this campaign eventually helped to compel a change in Belgrade's policy was later taken as some sort of vindication of air power acting alone.[6]

Yet the war in Kosovo was partly won on the ground – but not by NATO. The hints that NATO was contemplating an eventual land invasion may well have been instrumental in persuading Belgrade to withdraw, but the growing strength of the KLA was probably more important. The whole objective of the Serb campaign was to defeat the KLA and to deprive it of the population base required for sustained operations. But the ability of the KLA to grow in strength and confidence must have indicated to President Slobodan Milosevic that in the end he would lose Kosovo and that there was little point in taking even more pain from NATO air power. The unwillingness or inability to commit NATO troops had two important political consequences. First, it gave the Serbs the time and the space for ethnic cleansing, which was largely carried out by units barely inhibited by NATO airpower. Second, as NATO forces effectively followed it into Kosovo, the KLA acquired far more political clout and prestige than was commensurate with the alliance's pre-war Western political goals. This added to the demands on the post-war peacekeeping force, which soon looked to be set for a long stay.

Fighting the 'war on terror'
As the ultimate source of the 9/11 attacks, the choice of Afghanistan as a target was straightforward and relatively uncontroversial. Al-Qaeda had developed a symbiotic relationship with the Taliban regime and used the country as a headquarters and for training. The move to dislodge them in October 2001 began in a standard American pattern, with a strategic air campaign. This bore similarities to that in Bosnia in 1995 as well as Kosovo in 1999, with a focus on air defences, command networks and arms dumps, and occasional 'leadership' targets. But the infrastructure of Afghanistan was so wretched and primitive that there were few suitable targets to be attacked. What was the point of aiming for power plants in a country where only 6% of the population had electricity? Excessive bombing would risk doing no more than 'rearranging the sand', which was said to have been the main result of the cruise missile strikes against a supposed al-Qaeda conclave in Afghanistan in August 1998 after the attacks on the US embassies in East Africa. Unlike in the case of Kosovo,

there was no optimism that such a campaign could by itself achieve the strategic objective, which went beyond the coercive demands on Milosevic. There was still the same problem of meeting pre-war promises to avoid civilian casualties. It soon became apparent after one, largely unsuccessful, commando-type raid that such operations required far better logistics and intelligence than were available and that the air raids, after striking the few genuinely important targets, were doing more harm than good. The Afghan people were angry with the Americans because of civilian deaths, while the Taliban fighters were feeling even more confident because they had largely survived unscathed. If American troops came, as 'creatures of comfort', they would prove no match for fighters who had seen off much tougher Soviet soldiers.[7]

In late October, the US resorted to a lower-risk military strategy although this potentially carried greater political risks. Though relying on air power in isolation was not going to bring results, the United States was still not ready to commit substantial ground forces of its own to the campaign. Instead there was to be close cooperation with the anti-Taliban Northern Alliance. This involved putting to one side misgivings about the Alliance's combat capability as well as the narrowness of its political base. The Northern Alliance took on the crucial infantry role, playing a more substantial and explicit part than the KLA played in Kosovo, but with the same risks of awkward political associations. Now the air campaign had land operations to serve as a focus. As B-52s dropped 'dumb' bombs on the Taliban's forward positions the results were impressive. Almost as soon as the northern city of Mazar-e-Sharif fell, the fighting spirit of the Taliban appeared to evaporate, and a series of sharp advances backed by betrayals and defections did the rest. Soon Kabul fell and effectively the Taliban was defeated. Although, prior to the start of the air strikes, there had been many indications that the Pentagon understood that this time substantial ground forces might be required, in the event there was clear relief that they had not been necessary and that the US could chalk up, at least in its initial stages, another war virtually free of combat casualties.

After the cities had fallen, attention moved to the Tora Bora caves where a network of hiding places and passages had been prepared for sturdy defence. Here operations were far less successful. This was not territory in which the Northern Alliance was of much value and the coalition lacked the troops and local knowledge to hunt down the enemy. Osama bin Laden and his key lieutenants escaped into Pakistan. In December 2001, before the frustrations at Tora Bora, President George W. Bush suggested that a lesson of more general application had been learned. He spoke enthusiastically about the combination of 'real-time intelligence, local allied forces, special forces, and precision air power' that had produced a victory in the first round of the war, adding that this conflict 'has taught us more about the future of our military than a decade of blue ribbon panels and think tank symposiums'.[8] There were apparently few enemies that could not be battered into submission through the application of carefully targeted but also overwhelming air power, even while acknowledging that it worked best when used in conjunction with ground forces (preferably someone else's), which would oblige the enemy to occupy open positions, help to identify targets and to follow through after the bombing.

There was nothing exceptional in the combination of the post- and the pre-modern. The most effective irregular forces have always proved to be adept at borrowing the more advanced technologies when it suited them: witness the Mujahideen's use of *Stinger* anti-aircraft missiles to blunt Soviet air power in Afghanistan; or Hizbollah's ability to provide videos of their ambushes of Israeli units in Lebanon to the news media; or for that matter al-Qaeda's ability in September 2001 to mount an audacious attack by turning Western technology against itself, with knives acting as the force multiplier at the critical moment as aircraft were hijacked. Moreover, in practice an important factor in the swift success of the ground campaign was a tried and tested Afghan way of warfare, depending on coercive diplomacy, with protracted sparring to see who had superior power, before the hard bargaining began on the terms of surrender or, as likely, defection. US special forces may have had sophisticated new equipment to help them to operate in unfamiliar terrain, and the role played by UAVs in finding and even attacking targets was impressive, but a critical item in their armoury was large wads of dollars which could provide a formidable inducement to waverers. For those with the sense not to fight to the bitter end, defeat became rather like insolvency, with the faction in question soon trading under another name. Trading was often the operative word, for with territorial control came the ability to take a share of all economic activity, including trafficking in guns and drugs. Surrender was conditional: remarkably few Taliban fighters were disarmed and many appeared to have drifted back, still armed, to their villages or into banditry. So, while the Americans were relieved by the speed of the Taliban surrender, they did not always appreciate its conditional quality.

Also in late 2001, Deputy Secretary of Defense Paul Wolfowitz explained that 'one of the lessons of Afghanistan's history, which we've tried to apply in this campaign, is if you're a foreigner, try not to go in. If you do go in, don't stay too long, because they don't tend to like any foreigners who stay too long.'[9] In practice, an early departure was impossible. Despite itself, the United States soon learned that it had little choice but to get involved in nation-building. Initially it considered this a job for others, organised into an international force to help the new government to secure Kabul at least, while a separate force under its own command carried on hunting guerrillas and terrorists, even at the cost of undermining the stabilisation project. Eventually, more sensible and extensive arrangements were introduced, although valuable time had been lost.

The defeat of the Taliban regime and its al-Qaeda allies, in return for attacks launched from Afghanistan in the past, was followed by the defeat of Saddam Hussein's regime in 2003 for what might be launched from Iraq in the future. The move against Iraq was far more controversial. It was also described as a war of necessity and as part of the 'war on terror'. In building the domestic case, direct links between Saddam Hussein's regime and al-Qaeda, and even with the 9/11 attacks, were constantly asserted, although the evidence was flimsy. The international case was based on Iraqi non-compliance with a series of UN resolutions requiring the elimination of all WMD. The evidence here was stronger but still in vital respects overstated. The humanitarian advantage of getting rid of an evil regime was also cited, but not as the prime purpose. Only after the regime was overthrown and neither WMD nor real evidence of links with al-Qaeda had been found, did this humanitarian rationale come to the fore.

The initial 2003 Iraqi campaign was different from that of Afghanistan. There was no longer seen to be a need for an extended strategic air campaign. Nor was there a sufficiently strong local force to take on the Iraqis (other than the Kurds in their semi-autonomous northern territories). In consequence, coalition armies were engaged from the start. During the years since 1991, when strategy had been cautious, the gap between US and Iraqi forces had widened even further. It had then been assumed that intensive preparation of the battlefield was vital, by destroying from the air as many tanks and artillery pieces as possible, while scaring the ordinary troops into desertion and demoralisation. This was before coalition ground forces advanced. The speed with which Iraqi resistance crumbled in 1991 reduced the expectations for 2003. That war demonstrated just how overwhelming the air superiority of the US conventional forces had become. In 2003, initial progress was halting and gave some clues as to what was to come: no massive popular enthusiasm for the occupying forces, the use of guerrilla tactics by the coalition's opponents. Nevertheless, the combination of rapid manoeuvre and deadly air strikes soon proved irresistible and the regime's resistance crumbled. Any troop concentrations offered easy targets against which there was no reliable form of defence. Even acknowledging the enfeebled state of Iraqi forces, to occupy a country this size with only three divisions was remarkable. Soon, Saddam Hussein was in hiding. His sons were killed in an ambush and by the end of the year he had been dragged from a hole in the ground. The ruthless efficiency of the initial occupation was impressive and confirmed the complete superiority of the United States in conventional warfare.

The contrast with what followed was stark. While the major combat operations proved to be relatively undemanding, dealing with the insurgency that followed turned out to be both demanding and deadly, threatening to stretch out almost indefinitely. The Ba'ath regime may not ever have expected to be able to mount much conventional resistance prior to the war and always planned guerrilla warfare. This did not materialise in the fights for the major cities, including Baghdad, where a degree of urban warfare had been anticipated. It was only later, as the US mismanaged the post-war occupation, that the insurgency began to make itself felt. The qualitative superiority that allowed the US to defeat with ease the larger, although generally third-rate, Iraqi army meant that it lacked the numbers on the ground to establish its presence and to assert local authority after the war. Having begun with a legitimacy deficit, in terms of both domestic and international support for a war which was widely seen to have a contrived rationale, the US-led coalition struggled against an enemy as vicious as it was determined.

Just as Washington had overstated the threat posed by pre-war Iraq it had understated the problems of post-war Iraq.[10] The experience of Afghanistan at least encouraged some recognition that issues of reconstruction and nation-building could not be ducked, yet there was a degree of wishful thinking about the ease with which this deeply divided and brutalised society could settle on a new form of government. Even more seriously, the transition from an invading force to an occupying administration was poorly handled. In part, this was because preparations had been made to cope with the expected problem of hundreds of thousands of refugees, in flight from urban fighting, instead of the actual problem of a breakdown of law and order in the cities. More critically, there were simply too few troops. Secretary of Defense Donald Rumsfeld had made a point of demonstrating just how much could be achieved in modern warfare with remarkably few troops on the ground, but this meant ignoring all pre-war calculations that suggested that numbers in the region of 500,000 would be needed, rather than the 135,000 actually available. After Army Chief of Staff General Eric K. Shinseki advised that hundreds of thousands of troops might be needed, Wolfowitz observed that he found it 'hard to conceive that it would take more forces to provide stability in a post-Saddam Iraq than it would take to conduct the war itself and to secure the surrender of Saddam's security forces and his army'.[11]

This problem was exacerbated by the failure to hold the Iraqi army together (admittedly difficult as so many had deserted and the barracks had been destroyed). The process of building up competent Iraqi forces for internal security was thereafter slow and difficult. Lastly, those US troops available were not well trained for a post-war setting. They remained in 'force protection' mode and killed too many ordinary Iraqis. The point was made eloquently by a marine serving in central Iraq: 'If anyone gets too close to us we … waste them. It's kind of a shame, because it means we've killed a lot of innocent people.'[12] US troops became alienated from the Iraqi people, thereby helping their enemies to acquire recruits and local sanctuaries. This problem grew with the insurgency, in which the armed opposition was able to blend in with civilians and so undermine any hopes of developing trust between the Americans and the local population, especially in Sunni areas. The British, in the relatively more hospitable Shi'ite south and with more experience of this sort of situation, had fewer problems although they were unable to exercise much influence on local power struggles.

Immediately after 9/11, the US promised a new type of war as it sought to respond to a new type of threat. Yet have the campaigns in Afghanistan and Iraq really marked the anticipated break with the past? The attitude of the United States was certainly different. It was in an uncompromising mood, ready to take the military initiative, mobilising massive forces to do so and (at least rhetorically) accepting the sacrifices that the new campaigns might require. The wars were not presented as discretionary nor, initially, as humanitarian in purpose. They reflected the strategic imperatives of the new age of jihadist terror and so their legitimacy was derived from the demands of national security. The argument went that as the security of all civilised people was at risk from groups such as al-Qaeda, then all should join the campaign. At the same time, this was a matter of self-defence and there was no absolute requirement to find a sponsoring organisation. At most, the UN could take over occupied countries once the offending regimes had been overthrown. Not even NATO, however, could expect to influence the command and control of the military campaign. The war would be conducted by a coalition of the willing (mainly drawn from the 'Anglosphere' of the US, the UK and Australia) and on American terms.

Yet, although the 'war on terror' at first involved military operations of a somewhat old-fashioned variety, invading and occupying other countries against the wishes and resistance of the regimes in power, in other respects these operations could be seen as reinforcing the underlying trend. US forces found themselves having to cope with an enemy that intermingled with civil society, in wars that could not end with decisive battles but only with the collapse of political will. As the US 'will' had broken first in a number of relatively recent conflicts (Vietnam, Lebanon and Somalia), it was not unreasonable for its enemies (and potential friends) to suppose that this might break again.

Once the old order had been overthrown, the problems of establishing a new order led to demands on armed forces similar to those resulting from humanitarian interventions and, in particular, the need to create conditions for economic and political reconstruction by maintaining security against those who wished to disrupt this process. Moreover, the situations in Afghanistan and Iraq required the United States to take operations of this type seriously. In this respect, the 'war on terror' provided more and better reasons to become involved in the problems of distant parts of the third world. If these problems were ignored, these distant countries could well turn into breeding grounds for terrorism and sanctuaries for those plotting further attacks on the US and its allies. What may turn out to be more important than the content of new strategic priorities of the current decade is the mixed experience of their pursuit. The consequences of the invasion and occupation of Iraq in particular have raised major questions about military methodology and the legitimacy of the use of force.

Out of this experience comes a growing sense of the ideological as well as the operational aspects of contemporary conflict. These ideological aspects appear in many forms: as questions about the relationship between civil liberties and terrorist threats; the importance of 'hearts and minds' in a counter-insurgency campaign; how to engage with the different religious and political strands within the Islamic world; and whether censorious international opinion or disappointed allies really matter. One of the 'lessons learned' has been to recognise the importance and impact not only of ideas, but also of images. Some of these images, including the collapse of the Twin Towers in New York, the abuse of prisoners at Abu Ghraib, the long beard of Osama bin Laden and a haggard Saddam Hussein emerging from a hole in the ground, have developed an iconography all of their own. This suggests that a focus on the kinetic aspects of war must miss some of the more intriguing, difficult and significant features of contemporary conflict.

CHAPTER FIVE

Strategic Communications

The information environment

The ability to turn potentially hostile public opinion in one's favour, but also to retain the support of a home population, can be a vital strategic attribute. When efforts to this end fail it is tempting to blame the media for neglecting to draw salient facts to the public's attention, for passing on enemy propaganda and for deliberately misleading in pursuit of their own agendas. The importance of the media has increased because of our growing ability to collect and transmit images and words across continents. Governments and armed forces find that they must take this into account in their plans and practices, developing some sensitivity as to how past boasts might return to haunt them or casual cruelty might be broadcast around the world. The public disillusionment over Vietnam was often credited to the influence of the harsh portrayals of combat in the media, which picked up on the contradictions between official claims and the realities of the war on the ground. The sceptical attitude of journalists and broadcasters was a change from those of the previous generation who had accepted their role as a patriotic extension of the war effort. After Vietnam, policy-makers knew that they could never assume a respectful hearing, especially when events were taking a turn for the worse. In terms of the communication between the combat zone, the 'home front' and on to the wider international audience, the media's role was crucial.

Over the past two decades changing technology has recast the role of the media. In the Falklands in 1982, the British government was able to control reporting from the journalists with the Task Force, largely for logistical reasons. This has proved to be progressively more difficult in subsequent wars, as direct satellite links allow for more freelance operations by journalists. The military have had to learn to live with the consequences of the increasing openness of information, rather than developing a capacity for its denial. One day, they may successfully demonstrate their determination to ensure pin-point accuracy by showing videos of smart attacks on command centres. The next day, they may be responding to television footage of the human cost of another missile taking a wrong turning. The same television stations carry the claims of all sides in a conflict and, as a matter of course, now seem to show military operations from the perspective of both those launching them and those on the receiving end. Against this backdrop, governments and military commanders are bound to put considerable effort into describing, explaining and justifying operations. The ground might be prepared by feeding snippets of information, and operations may be timed with television schedules in mind. Spokespersons will need to avoid appearing unaware of blunders by their own side or risk being caught out in self-contradiction. A charismatic commander will be encouraged to help to convince a sceptical public as much as to boost the morale of front-line troops. And so military operations have come to be understood in terms of the stories they tell as much as their direct impact on the enemy's physical capacity. The broadcasting media will transmit 'breaking news' far faster than most government systems and so operational secrecy in modern limited wars now requires their active connivance. Even a sudden news blackout from a particular base or aircraft carrier can be extraordinarily telling, a sure indication that something significant is underway. Aspects of this would have been intolerable to previous generations of military commanders – especially those who considered themselves at risk of defeat, allowing for no margin of error. If commanders can feel relaxed about this new situation, it is because they are working within comfortable margins. The superiority of Western forces in regular war means that they can allow the media much more latitude and, indeed, give them even more facilities because images of overwhelming and irresistible power will add to the coercive effect of their capabilities. When it comes to irregular warfare, the opportunities that the diffusion of the technologies for collecting and distributing information give to small groups of highly motivated individuals have created a different set of problems.

As the modern media have become increasingly competitive and dispersed, an additional twist has been added by the rise of the internet. High-quality material on almost anything can be found on the internet using free search engines. For a low price it is possible to get the sort of satellite images and navigational guidance that would once have been available only to the armed forces. Easy and uncontrollable forms of global and instantaneous communication have exponentially increased the number of actors able to shape the narrative. Pictures and videos of important events are as likely to be taken by passers-by or by people involved in the action on mobile phone cameras, as by commissioned professionals. This provides a major opportunity for pressure groups and political activists to shape perceptions by providing the media with images of their activities or those they wish to expose.

This new information environment has had important political effects and created new strategic options. In theory, taken as a whole, the information revolution ought to work more to the detriment of closed than open societies, just as when information was scarce and controllable it could be used for elitist purposes. Many of the early advances in communications, such as the radio, were seen as natural instruments of totalitarianism. Radio released individuals from dependence upon local sources of knowledge, thereby diminishing at a stroke traditional sources of authority and creating a 'mass society', reliant on externally generated news which could be controlled by a central authority. The masses need hear only one voice and this voice would be inescapable. This same central authority would be able to monitor loose talk and subversive action. This was the grim vision of George Orwell's 1984, in which Big Brother controlled the information environment. It did not work out that way because no country could ever be sealed off from external influences. In the end, the most vulnerable points of the Soviet system turned out to be its inability to block broadcasts of the BBC World Service and the Voice of America or to prevent the intrusion into Soviet and East European homes of Western television programmes that undermined the official line simply by demonstrating an alternative. This did not require any overt political message.

The opportunities for political subversion through information flows that are hard to detect and prevent have grown with each technological innovation. Thus audio tapes were employed during the 1978 overthrow of the Shah of Iran, videotapes in the Philippine 'People Power' revolution of 1986 and fax machines in the campaign against Panama's General Manuel Noriega in the late 1970s.[1] It is now harder than ever before to keep society sealed off from external influences, although governments continue to try. When the Mexican government moved against the Zapatistas in 1994, the rebels used laptops to issue commands and the internet to publicise allegations of government atrocities to gain support from international organisations. Increasingly, no special effort is required to transmit video and audio material through the internet. Yet authoritarian governments have not all buckled under this weight. The contest between the free-flow of information and authoritarian regimes is currently at its most intense in China, which has developed the world's most sophisticated internet filtering system, seeking to prevent access to pornography, religious material and political dissent. This effort is bolstered by both legal regulation and technical control, involving thousands of personnel censoring communications including web pages, online discussion forums and email messages. Cybercafés are required by law to track internet usage by their customers and to keep records.[2] Even the search engines which symbolise the promise of democratic access to information, such as Yahoo and Google, have compromised their principles in order to secure market access to China. The Chinese system is generally considered to be successful and a model for those who wish to maintain a monopoly of political power. How successful this effort can be in the longer term, especially as China engages intensely with the international economy and its citizens travel the world, remains to be seen. The answer, as is normally the case, probably depends on the extent of the social and political stresses and strains developing in society for other reasons. This is an issue of demand as much as supply, of a hunger for news and ideas that can explain unfolding events and suggest effective ways forward, and a readiness to take risks and to affront the authorities in the search for this material.

In the more open societies of the West, the new means of communication are a formidable weapon in the hands of the disaffected and alienated. They facilitate the development and spread of alternative world-views that are able to challenge what are presented to be malign, incredible and, therefore, mendacious mainstream views. One of the striking things about al-Qaeda is its combination of a fundamentalist theology, which pits itself against modernity (its ally the Taliban banned television), and a readiness to exploit the possibilities of the revolution in communications technology to the full. Bin Laden's group was among the first to use commercial satellite telephones and to produce propaganda videos with hand-held cameras. Their fighters were reported to be retreating from Afghanistan carrying laptops as well as Kalashnikovs. At first, al-Qaeda, with its followers, associates and imitators, used the internet to build, indoctrinate and inspire support. Eventually it came to be used for more activist purposes. Young militants are as likely to be found in anonymous cybercafés as in training camps abroad, following message boards, taking instruction in bomb-making, sniping and how to move across international borders, or even watching snuff videos from Iraq.

Teenagers in the cities of northern England can be inspired by the hardened veterans of campaigns in Chechnya and Kashmir. Just like enthusiasts for eccentric hobbies and unusual sports, they can meet like-minded individuals through the internet and agree to work together. In their plans at least they are no longer constrained by time and space. Their communications can be encrypted, carried in numerous languages or just lost in the billions of every-day communications beyond the scope of monitoring agencies. At the time of the 9/11 attacks one source had identified 12 jihadist websites; four years later the figure was 4,500 sites, representing a virtual 'community of belief' or 'one big *madrassa*'. Discussions of strategy and plans, and even technical instruction, can take place in sanctuary conditions.[3] The internet allows pressure groups and individuals to reach mass audiences far more directly than before without the mediating influence of the mass media. A starting point of engagement can be described and interpreted through extensive networks of activists and sympathisers. Once the raw material is present in this network, a political critical mass can be created at the press of an 'enter' key.

Media battles

The ability to take advantage of this new information environment is now considered to be an essential attribute in contemporary conflicts. Jean Seaton observed with regard to Kosovo that the 'media and public opinion are the territory in which the battle for intervention is fought'.[4] As one commentator on the role of narratives in US domestic politics observed that, as a result of Iraq 'foreign policy and even warfare itself has moved its central locality from the battlefield to the narrative on the airwaves and internet'. Matt Stoller argues that although previous conflicts were media-driven, 'the battlefield dictated the spin'. Now, he claims, the spin drives the conflict, whether targeted at Iraqis, Americans or Europeans.[5] Perhaps the most eloquent testimony to the importance of these issues came in the rather pained July 2005 letter purported to come from Osama bin Laden's lieutenant, Ayman al-Zawahiri, to Abu Musab al-Zarqawi, the Jordanian leader of the Iraqi insurgency. In this letter, Zawahiri stresses the importance of public support in the Muslim world, and notes how it might be turned off by attacks on mosques, even though they are Shi'ite rather than Sunni, and by video beheadings of kidnapped Westerners:

> I say to you: that we are in a battle, and that more than half of this battle is taking place in the battlefield of the media. And that we are in a media battle in a race for the hearts and minds of our Umma.[6]

If a regular battle is won then the results can be measured in casualties and territory. Measuring the results of a narrative or media battle is much more difficult. The media often declares a victor on the basis of what are essentially media values – slick presentation, fluency, a steady diet of new stories, avoiding getting caught in embarrassing contradictions. Such evaluations may be more about how the message is packaged rather than the message itself. It would be unwise to dismiss the importance of packaging, but many audiences may be more forgiving of an amateurish approach if that gives them greater confidence in the integrity of the message. More seriously, audiences are likely to test the message by reference to their own experience and established belief systems. Indeed, success in a narrative battle lies in changing these belief systems so that significant sections of the population start to see the developing conflict in a different light. Given the resilience of belief systems this may be no small matter. Even if this is achieved, then there still have to be consequences. People have to act differently and these actions must have consequences in turn.

For example, the possibility that Western governments might be moved by the suffering of the victims of aggression has influenced the strategies of those seeking to draw Western states into conflicts from which they might normally have expected to steer clear, and also of those seeking to keep them out. Those who have the upper hand will want to persuade outsiders not to meddle; those losing out will be searching for ways to suck outsiders in. There is nothing novel about belligerents conducting their affairs with one eye on the possibilities of others joining in, seeking alliances on the one hand, and declarations of neutrality on the other. For those encouraging intervention, the key message to communicate would be that they could not cope on their own and risked being overwhelmed by a ruthless enemy careless of human life. The advantage of a victim strategy was illustrated early in the wars of the former Yugoslavia. In August 1991, Serb forces began a three-month siege of the Croatian town of Vukovar, with 45,000 inhabitants, which eventually took the lives of more than 2,000 people and reduced the city to rubble. While this was underway, Serb forces took a third of Croatia's territory, even though Serbs represented just over 12% of the population. The international media soon picked up on the images of distressed people being shelled out of their homes. In these circumstances, 'media manipulation became not so much a complement for military engagement as a substitute for it'.[7] The government in Zagreb made no attempt to defend Vukovar, sending minimal material support. The strategy worked: mounting indignation, not least in Germany, meant that international pressure was put on the Serbs and Croatian independence was recognised. Although the Bosnian government did not initially follow a victim strategy, eventually it had few options. As the conflict deepened, along with the human tragedy it engendered, Sarajevo worked to shame the international community into sorting out the mess, or at least into giving the Bosnian government the wherewithal to do it itself. It was alleged that incidents were staged in order to stimulate Western interest in the Bosnian Muslims' plight.[8]

Governments which are minded to do so can resist such media-reliant campaigns. It is only when they are uncertain about what policy line to take or start to have doubts about the direction policy has taken that they will allow themselves to be influenced strongly by mainstream media, let alone internet campaigns. As the late Peter Jennings of ABC Television insisted: 'political leadership trumps good television every time'.[9] The readiness of the American and British governments to persevere in Iraq, despite a lack of international support and a decline in domestic support, indicates the limits of both a hostile media and disenchanted public opinion. There is always the argument that the ballot box is the place where public support should be tested and both these governments won elections post-Iraq.

Nonetheless, assumptions about the impact of the media become part of the narrative itself: governments start to factor into their thinking the possibility that images revealing large-scale suffering may push them into 'doing something', while images exposing the cost of that 'something' may impede action. And governmental resolve is not always so firm. As wars of choice, the humanitarian interventions of the 1990s always appeared dependent on fragile public support that might applaud an operation to relieve suffering but then could be turned by bad news or doubts about where operations were leading. The idea of the 'CNN effect' conveyed concerns that viewers might be so touched by images of desperate humanity that they would demand action, even in quite inappropriate circumstances. This was said to be relevant to the American intervention in Somalia in December 1992. 'How can ifs and buts compete', wrote one columnist, 'with the image of a mother and child dying before our eyes?'[10] The novelty, observed British Foreign Secretary Douglas Hurd, lay not in 'mass rape, the shooting of civilians, in war crimes, in ethnic cleansing, in the burning of towns and villages', but 'that a selection of these tragedies is now visible within hours to people around the world. People reject and resent what is going on because they know it more visibly than before.'[11] However, that the idea that strong images or descriptions of suffering could be of sufficient eloquence to generate policy is not supported by the evidence. Attempts to pin down the CNN effect have yet to prove its existence.[12] The example of the gassing of Kurds in the city of Halabjah by Iraqi forces in 1988, as part of a vicious campaign being waged by Saddam Hussein. This was well reported at the time, but Western governments were then attempting to develop a policy of constructive engagement with Iraq and so chose not to make a fuss. In other circumstances, when the objective was to encourage action, this atrocity would have been highlighted by every official spokesman. This illustrates the extent to which governments are not just the recipients of strong story lines developed in the media, but work hard to insert their own constructions on events into public debate in order to garner support for policies.

Although the decisions of democratically elected governments can claim a natural legitimacy, they prefer to be working with public opinion and are apt to become nervous if they have failed to persuade international opinion. The legitimacy of a military operation is a subjective attribute, related to questions of legality and morality as well as security. Because it is subjective this is an area where the inability to develop persuasive narratives about the whys and wherefores of a controversial policy will make itself felt. An operation's legitimacy will be hard to obtain and sustain if it is not in accord with the prevailing political culture, and in the West, that means with liberal values. Western forces should not engage in gratuitous cruelty; military actions must be clearly linked to a realisable political purpose. The wider international community will judge the application of force by high standards and expects that every effort would be made to keep both civilian and military casualties to a minimum. For any operational move there will be a number of different audiences beyond the immediate combatants. The course of the fighting will be followed closely by those who have a stake in its outcome, including international organisations, and as the fighting becomes intense and difficult it will become a matter of intense speculation, agitating and exciting the international media and internet bloggers alike.

There will always be an argument that military actions that might make Western opinion uncomfortable might still be vital if the enemy is to be defeated. For though any use of violent methods is bound to lead to unease, if the cause is adopted as just, then these methods might be tolerated as unavoidable. Against this claim that desperate times require desperate measures, it will be argued that such measures directed at civilians, such as air raids, or rough and ready forms of interrogation, are not only ethically dubious but militarily pointless or even counter-productive. It is normally claimed, for example, that civilian populations are hard to coerce through strategic bombing or that little information of any reliability emerges through torture. This may well be true, although there will still be exceptions, where threats to populations or to individuals will result in their wills breaking.

The only real test of restraint as a matter of principle in these areas is in those cases where there might be reason to suppose that real benefits could result from extreme coercive measures. Even so, they will still be damaging because revelations of such behaviour will undermine confidence in and respect for the values and conduct of Western countries. A strategy based on a commitment to liberal values may well involve operational penalties: against these must be put the advantages of being able to avoid divisive debates about extreme tactics and to draw upon broader sources of support.

Hearts and minds

The reason why these battles are assumed to make a difference in irregular war is that the conduct of such wars depends on the attitudes of ordinary civilians for the provision of recruits, sustenance and shelter, and these attitudes might well be subject to private change. In regular war, the morale of ordinary soldiers can be a target, but they will be subject to military discipline and so any major changes in attitudes will take time before they have an effect.

Few phrases sum up the target of this battle more than 'hearts and minds'. It has been part of common parlance since it was first used extensively in Vietnam.[13] It is referred to whenever questioning harsh methods used by one's own side and whenever there is a need to persuade people, through good works and sensitivity to their concerns, that the government and the security forces are really on their side. It sums up the idea of wars being won in the cognitive rather than the physical domain. It supports an essential counter-insurgency, and counter-terrorism, strategy by suggesting a way of winning over a population that might otherwise be hostile (and which subjected to brute force almost certainly will be), thereby depriving militant opponents of their potential sources of backing.

It may be possible, as Israel has demonstrated, to box in and hold down a hostile population. It has coped with the second intifada by setting barriers to movement and engaging in selective assassination. But while such tactics may work to contain the anger of people under occupation, they cannot be the basis for governing them. Tough action is more likely, at least in the short term, to forge links between the militants and the wider population than to break the resistance, although it is often rationalised on the assumption that reliably punitive retaliation will encourage the relatively uncommitted segments of the population to back off. Such coercive strategies tend to be favoured when much political ground has already been lost, along with local hearts and minds. An example of this turn came in April 2004, when the deliberately provocative murder of four American contractors in the Iraqi city of Fallujah by Sunni militants led to a tough American urban offensive. By way of symbolising the change of attitude, Robert D. Kaplan reports meeting up with US marines prior to the Fallujah battle and finding them sporting moustaches to identify with the local population; when they prepared for the battle, angry at recent events, they shaved them off.[14] According to British Army Brigadier Nigel Aylwin-Foster, the insurgent action was designed to create a disproportionate response and in this it was successful. The American anger led to a 'kinetic' rather than a strategic response, which, in the event, was not followed through to its logical conclusion because of the evident political backlash that resulted. Aylwin-Foster suggests that the inclination to intimidate opponents rather than to win over waverers has been a feature of pacification operations in Iraq. One analysis that he cites of operations conducted from 2003 to 2005 notes that most were 'reactive to insurgent activity – seeking to hunt down insurgents. Only 6% of ops were directed specifically to create a secure environment for the population.' Unfortunately the damaging political consequences of these actions were not always appreciated. Because the cause was just, it was assumed that the actions would be understood even when they resulted in tragic errors.[15]

The strategy of search and destroy (or 'cordon and sweep' in Iraq) reflects the familiar military view that ultimately physical force is all that matters in war, that the basic objective is to hold territory and to kill the enemy, gaining respect if not love. This approach did not, however, fare that well in Vietnam either: it was always easier to destroy than to search, and the indiscriminate nature of the destruction served to antagonise the local population and so to add to the stock of militants. Military operations are judged only by their presumed military effects and not their political ones. It is, of course, much harder to train soldiers to withhold fire, not to rise to provocations and to reach out to a wary local population when this might put them in danger. When nerves are frayed it does not take much to turn a tense encounter into a vicious fire-fight with profound political consequences.

Montgomery McFate, with the unusual status of a cultural anthropologist working for the Pentagon, has identified three examples of mistakes in Iraq that resulted from a lack of appreciation of Iraqi culture. First was a failure to grasp that the civilian apparatus of the country would not survive the loss of the regime as power would revert to the tribes; second, there was a presumption that key communications would flow through the broadcast media rather than coffee-shop rumours (and US force protection doctrine meant that coffee shops were out of bounds); third, an Iraqi propensity to get physically close to those they were addressing was found threatening by American troops, while the hand gestures for stop were reversed in the American and Iraqi cultures, leading to tragic misunderstandings at road blocks.[16] Yet, in other respects, common sense as much as deep cultural awareness is required. In his trenchant critique of US Army counter-insurgency operations, Aylwin-Foster described the requirements of successful operations, different from those required for conventional warfighting, as the ability to 'see issues and actions from the perspective of the domestic population' and 'how easily excessive force, even when apparently justified, can undermine popular support'.[17]

The difficulties faced in Iraq have led to soul-searching within the US Army. Whereas after Vietnam the army recovered through a rediscovery of the operational art of major war, that option is not available now. The commitments in Afghanistan and Iraq cannot be readily abandoned and those officers coming through their tours of duty have been made painfully aware of the inadequacy of prior preparations for these conflicts and the need to do better next time. They realise that they have been trained to shoot, but less well how to cope with crowds, to maintain contact with local dignitaries and to distribute food. At the Army's Command and General Staff College all students are being instructed in counter-insurgency. At the 'elite School of Advanced Military Studies … 31 of 78 student monographs this year were devoted to counterinsurgency or "stability operations", compared with "only a couple" two years ago'. A new manual on counter-insurgency operations is being written, with input from the British army. One officer has been quoted as saying: 'We used to say that if you could do the war fighting, the other stuff was a lesser included case. What we've learned the hard way is that the other stuff is much more difficult.'[18] Major-General Robert H. Scales, Jr, in developing his theme of culture-centric warfare, has argued the need for 'a cadre of global scouts, well educated, with a penchant for languages and a comfort with strange and distant places. These soldiers should be given time to absorb a single culture and to establish trust with those willing to trust them.'[19]

When conducting counter-insurgency operations, heightened cultural awareness is not essential to realise that arbitrary arrests, displays of brute force, rudeness and disrespectful behaviour are likely to generate alienation and hostility. Reactions to being treated harshly and disdainfully for no good reason, especially by uninvited foreign troops, are not likely to vary greatly among otherwise diverse cultures. In the aftermath of such behaviour, repairing the damage and putting a positive 'spin' on events requires more than a keen and well-resourced public affairs outfit but rather evidence that policies have been changed and more appropriate behaviour is now in place.

A simple switch to a hearts and minds strategy approach may not, however, be the answer. This is because while it is clear what it does not involve, in terms of avoiding provocative military action, its more active features are less clear. In fact the term itself requires some unpacking. Just as search and destroy are not always in harmony, nor are hearts and minds. In other contexts, heart and mind are often pitted against each other – strong emotions versus cool calculation, appeals to values and symbols versus appeals to the intellect. In strategic discourse, much hearts and minds theory seems very hearts oriented, as if by showing a human face with a ready smile, with desperately needed goods and services being brought by Sergeant Bountiful backed up by Major Reassurance, a thankful but hitherto sullen populace can be won over. Such activities can undoubtedly have substantial payoffs, but only in favourable conditions. This points to two important limitations of the approach.

First, they must address the real concerns and grievances of the local people. The failure of the hearts and minds approach in Vietnam (some say it was never really given a chance before it was discarded) was because its purposes were subverted to serve the needs of the South Vietnamese regime rather than the people. That is, to succeed it has to be passingly democratic and this may well upset local power structures. In part it may be a matter of civic action, repairing roads and building schools, or making securing power and sanitation infrastructures, but at some point issues of official repression, land reform or ethnic mix may become germane. Daniel Byman observes how, in the war against terror, the allies of the US:

> are often the source of the problem as well as the heart of any solution … The nature of regimes and of societies feeds an insurgency, but the United States is often hostage to its narrow goals with regard to counterinsurgency and thus becomes complicit in the host-nation's self-defeating behavior.[20]

If the sources of discontent are to be found in the local power structure, an effective strategy may require acting as a radical, even subversive local force. This can be a difficult manoeuvre when continued presence depends on the support of the local elites. Alternatively, as the British have found in southern Iraq, where there is something of a political vacuum, non-provocative action can mean conceding the political initiative to local gangs and militias.

Second, there is a chicken-and-egg problem, because these strategies can be too dangerous to follow without local security, until local security is established they cannot be followed. Without security, foreign troops and local people will be unable to interact closely and to develop mutual trust. Security is not just a matter of immediate safety: it also requires a look forward, assessing the likely future power structure that will emerge as the conflict develops and will probably be in place when the foreign troops leave. In this respect, a more minds-oriented approach must establish trust by addressing questions about who is likely to prevail in the continuing political and military struggle and the nature of the long-term political agendas of all involved. The insurgent can sow doubts as to the trustworthiness of the local population, about what is real and what is fake, as to who is truly on one's side and who is pretending. As the insurgents and counter-insurgents play mind games to gain local support, they may be as anxious to create impressions of strength as of kindness, to demonstrate a likely victory, as well as largesse.

Strategic communication

These problems are faced at the macro- as well as the micro-level. Embedded beliefs are difficult to dislodge and doing so is more than a matter of presentation. Even before the Iraq War of 2003, opinion polls were recording highly unfavourable views of the United States, including in supposedly allied countries such as Saudi Arabia and Kuwait. After the war, around the world, support for American policies was at an all-time low. Since then, and despite efforts to turn the tide, matters have barely improved.[21] After years of playing down the importance of public diplomacy and strategic communications, the US government has recently shown increased interest in them. 'Public diplomacy' is now defined as 'government-sponsored programs intended to inform or influence public opinion in other countries'. This is in contrast to normal diplomacy which is government-to-government and often kept as confidential as possible.[22] Byman warns that 'al-Qaeda is winning the battle of ideas'. Accordingly: 'Public diplomacy should try to offer a competing narrative, one that plays up the friendlier side of U.S. foreign policy and justifies less popular aspects.'[23]

In an article in the *Wall Street Journal* in July 2005, Donald Rumsfeld described how the Pentagon was working to adapt to the new realities of the information age. As successes, he cited the embedding of hundreds of reporters in US military units in *Operation Iraqi Freedom*, with few restrictions on what they could broadcast or publish, and the increasing amounts of information posted on the department's web pages, including material relevant to allegations of detainee abuse. The challenge of conveying accurate and complete information was multiplied, he noted, 'when it comes to the battle of perceptions beyond our borders'.[24] In February 2006 he complained to the Council on Foreign Relations that:

> Our enemies have skillfully adapted to fighting wars in today's media age, but for the most part we, our country, our government, has not adapted. Consider that the violent extremists have established media relations committees—these are terrorists and they have media relations committees that meet and talk about strategy, not with bullets but with words. They've proven to be highly successful at manipulating the opinion elites of the world. They plan and design their headline-grabbing attacks using every means of communication to intimidate and break the collective will of free people.
>
> They know that communications transcend borders and that a single news story handled skillfully can be as damaging to our cause and helpful to theirs as any other method of military attack. And they're doing it. They're able to act quickly. They have relatively few people. They have modest resources compared to the vast and expensive bureaucracies of Western governments.
>
> Our federal government is really only beginning to adapt our operations to the 21st century. For the most part, the U.S. government still functions as a five and dime store in an eBay world. Today we're engaged in the first war in history—unconventional and irregular as it may be—in an era of e-mails, blogs, cell phones, Blackberrys, Instant Messaging, digital cameras, a global Internet with no inhibitions, cell phones, hand-held video cameras, talk radio, 24-hour news broadcasts, satellite television. There's never been a war fought in this environment before.[25]

The difficulty the US exhibits when dealing with this situation is evident in the search for an appropriate language to describe the conflict. William Safire has noted how uncomfortable the Bush administration has appeared with the word 'insurgents' because of its connotation of 'admirable "underdogs" in a struggle against the established order or entrenched leadership', rather than enemies of a legitimate government, and also because it suggests that the disparate elements engaged in Iraq are more unified than is the case. Thus Bush, in preference to a single term, has referred to 'a combination of rejectionists, Saddamists and terrorists'. The previous category of 'Saddam loyalists' had been shortened to remove reference to an attribute – loyalty – that might be seen as positive by resentful Sunnis.[26] Another example of efforts at finding the language to build a compelling narrative came with the attempt to fill a gap by describing a strategy for Iraq. Contrary to what might have been expected, this was not the result of full discussions with local commanders. The aim was rather to explain matters to the American people to ensure that they did not come to favour a precipitate withdrawal. After Peter Feaver of Duke University presented an analysis which suggested that US public opinion would support the Iraq war, despite mounting casualties, if they believed it would ultimately succeed, he was recruited to work in the White House. Feaver was credited with drafting the administration's *Our National Strategy for Victory in Iraq*, released in December 2005. Hence the constant repetition of the word 'victory' in the president's speech launching the document.[27]

A far more serious challenge was in Iraq itself. There are now some 200 Iraqi-owned newspapers and 15 to 17 Iraqi-owned television stations. In Afghanistan there are some 350 magazines and newspapers and 68 television and radio stations. Some of these are supported financially by the US (often quite openly to encourage democracy). In other cases, inducements have been given to encourage various outlets to take stories that have been written under official US guidance but are published without attribution. Whatever the accuracy of such stories, they are almost bound to have a positive and upbeat theme and it may not require great insight to guess their provenance. When covert, propagandistic activities, involving large sums of money, are eventually disclosed in the US press, then the net effect is not only to discredit the 'news' stories that have been planted, but also the government for attempting to manipulate the media.[28] The pictures of torture at Abu Ghraib were undoubtedly a public relations disaster for the United States, because they provided vivid portrayals of matters which had previously been alluded to in print. It soon became evident that the behaviour they were portraying was real, widespread and a consequence, even if unintended, of high-level decisions. Because they were in stark contrast to the claims the US had made about itself, and the contrast it was trying to draw with the old Iraqi regime, the images were not easy to explain away. This case demonstrated how difficult it is for a government, especially one viewed with such suspicion as America is, to find ways of turning the tide of foreign opinion. Where it has been done, marginally, is where the US has demonstrated that it can act effectively in response to a humanitarian crisis, as in the cases of the 26 December 2004 tsunami and the October 2005 Pakistan earthquake.

Networks and hierarchies

The other role that might be played by a strategic narrative relates less to persuading a wavering opinion but in providing guidance for those already committed. This relates to the claim that information technology allows for an extremely dense communication net, thereby supporting networking types of organisation while making life difficult for other more hierarchical forms. In this context, a strategic narrative that helps with the appreciation of a situation and suggests courses of action can act almost as a substitute for normal command and control. So long as the core norms and values are internalised, and a particular analysis accepted, then there is no need to issue orders. This is then said (for example by the 'fourth-generation school', as discussed in chapter one) to create new possibilities for irregular warfare, as it helps dispersed, perhaps quite small, groups to coordinate their activities even without any formal organisation. The lack of central leadership means that a 'decapitation' attack is impossible. This can also be turned into an argument for flatter organisational structures in Western armed forces.

These claims need to be treated with some care. Fighting networks rather than hierarchies has been compared to playing the Chinese game of 'Go' rather than chess. Terrorists, insurgents or even non-violent radical groups do not need to rely on frontal assaults and hierarchical command chains but can 'swarm', advancing in small groups from many different directions and using different methods, in a network held together by mobile phones and the web. Such swarming certainly makes it difficult for governments to know quite what the arguments they are trying to contest are and renders them vulnerable to media ambush or, in the case of guerrilla warfare and terrorism, real ambush. The novelty of such tactics and their inherent advantages should not be overstated. It is quite natural for radical groups, especially during their early stages, to be based on loose networks of individuals. To the extent that they risk attracting the attention of the authorities they find it safer to operate as semi-independent cells, communicating with each other and their shared leadership as little as possible. To be sure, the internet and other forms of digitised communication make it easier to keep in touch, but the number of security breaches attributed to mobile phones must make them hesitant about talking too openly or too specifically. At any rate, in the past, even when the key forms of communication were pamphlets and public meetings, 'communities of belief' often developed, as demonstrated by religious sects and radical movements. In this respect, Marxism was a fabulous example of a strategic narrative that sustained countless political groups, from successful revolutionary parties to fringe 'groupscules'. Radical Islam can perform a similar function, with a basic message that is widely shared and capable of being disseminated by a variety of means.

Such narratives enable these groups to hold together; they help them to gather new adherents and to unnerve opponents. Indeed, without the narratives they would be pointless and there would be no purpose to the association. A more critical question, however, is whether they can enable these groups to move beyond the cellular form. When numerically weak and out-gunned, it helps to be dispersed and to operate in quite small cells. In this form they can score occasional tactical successes. If one cell goes down, then another can still continue with the struggle. When prominent targets and themes present themselves they can swarm around them, adding to the security concerns of governments and picking up on the unpopularity of certain policies. But if they never move beyond that point then they cannot progress politically. The great theorists of guerrilla warfare, such as Mao Zedong, were always clear that their objective was to create the conditions for a more decisive clash, in the demoralisation of the enemy and the desertion of its troops, and in the growing confidence and consciousness of the movement's supporters.

This was because the aim was to seize control of the state, the formal structures of power and in particular the means of organised violence. This required the sort of leadership that could see and then seize the opportunities to mobilise sufficient force to strike the decisive blows. Successful guerrilla groups are those that are able to turn themselves into conventional forces capable of occupying capital cities and install-ing governments. Even with chaotic revolutionary processes at play, at some point an assertive leadership would set the revolution on its new course. Thus Lenin made his push for power months after the fall of the Tsar, while the Ayatollah Khomeini was not really able to turn Iran into an Islamic Republic after the Shah's departure until he could see off the competing claims of liberal constitutionalists and sundry leftists. It is difficult to move beyond being a nuisance and harassing the enemy to seizing control without an authoritative point of decision.

If, as argued in the introduction to this paper, strategy is about the creation of power, then at some point it is also bound to be hierarchical. Many organisations could usefully work with flatter hierarchies: few can cope if they are totally flat. Priorities will still have to be set, resources allocated and an overview of a developing situation established. The information that allows for the horizontal integration of disparate groups and activities can also reinforce vertical integration, and this will enable the successful strategist to develop and communicate a coherent set of policies, to allocate resources in the most effective manner, to shift the weight of activity from one front to another and to choose measures most appropriate to the task in hand. In practice, political leaders and military commanders who are most effective and less reliant on formal chains of command are those with a natural authority and a message that is understood and readily communicated without having to be spelled out in detail to subordinates. It is inherent in irregular warfare that vital decisions, potentially with huge strategic consequences, have to be taken at a unit or even individual level. By their very nature, however, especially when risks are being taken with the lives of troops or apparently innocent civilians, these decisions are likely to draw in senior commanders and central government. Calming local demonstrations, taking prisoners, attacking supposed terrorist hideouts can all have major repercussions if poorly handled. Again, this reinforces the requirement for forms of communication down the lines of command that go beyond rules of engagement and specific orders and encourage a clear understanding of the stakes in the conflict and the expectations this creates for individual behaviour.

The role of strategic narratives in irregular warfare is therefore to provide a framework of understanding that can bind a fighting force together. By providing a strategic context it should guide tactical decisions. If this is the case then the challenge for counter-insurgency and counter-terrorism operations is to seek to unbind the enemy force by undermining the strategic narratives. This requires playing on the natural fault lines within the political movements that spawn terrorist groups in order to aggravate their differences. Such an approach is helped by the familiar tendency of radical movements to fragment into competing factions. These movements are not inherently pragmatic. They deal in ultimate ends and so small divisions over political programmes or current tactics can quickly be magnified into fundamental differences of principle. Those of a certain political generation will recall endless, pointless debates among competing socialist factions, often quite tiny, about obscure questions of Marxist–Leninist theory. Such an approach can consider itself successful so long as the insurgents or terrorists are prevented from moving beyond their networked, cellular form. If the enemy is not making progress it is apt to get frustrated with intense, internal strategic debates, with some arguing for more dramatic military actions to attract more attention and recruits, while others will argue the need for patient political work to develop a constituency. These disagreements may be personalised and factionalised and it could happen that these schisms reach such an intensity that the factions begin to fight.

There are numerous indications that such arguments are already raging among al-Qaeda and its affiliates. These debates are about both internal rivalries and strategic directions. They concern questions such as: is this movement engaged in a series of national campaigns which need to be won on their own terms or must the focus remain at all times on the global struggle? Are there not dangers in a sectarian stance when there might be opportunities to reach out to all strands of Islam? Are there innocents in this struggle or is anybody, however young or infirm, a legitimate casualty? Would it not be wiser to concentrate on the enemy elite and those who help them to stay in power? These debates are evident in the intercepted letter, already cited on p. 77, from al-Zawahiri to al-Zarqawi. The old guard can also see al-Zarqawi taking over their leadership role. His methods may inspire fear and a sort of respect, but might even lead to some soul-searching among those jihadists who train to take up the fight against crusaders and Zionists and then find themselves blowing up mosques and wedding parties. Doubts in the ranks lead to operational problems and even intelligence windfalls for the authorities. Once it is known that a group has informers in its midst and has been compromised, internal suspicions grow and capabilities are further reduced. It would, of course, be unwise to rely on such processes causing jihadist groups to implode. But it would be equally unwise to ignore the basic point that terrorists believe that they are acting strategically, and that attacks on their strategies, demonstrating their ultimate futility as well as their obnoxious morality, can undermine both their confidence and capabilities.

Contemporary circumstances give insurgents and terrorists tactical opportunities that they would have lacked in previous eras. They can plot and act on a global scale, and when they do so successfully they can cause the enormous dislocation of whole societies. The costs involved in mounting operations can be met from an individual's budget, while the economic costs inflicted can reach billions of dollars. Suicidal methods have an alarming multiplier effect on the likelihood of attacks succeeding and the resulting casualties. Participation in such atrocities holds an appeal for a substantial number of people and many more may cheer them on. For all these reasons, preventing terrorist attacks and mitigating their consequences should they occur has become a high priority for governments. Yet the strategic achievements of this activity have been meagre. A number of attacks have been thwarted and where they have succeeded the political effects have either been marginal or counter-productive to their cause.

Only in Iraq itself has an effective campaign been developed. In the chaos following the overthrow of Saddam's regime, opportunities were created for the insurgents and a critical mass of activists came into being. There are divisions among the various groups on both objectives and methods. As the most extreme base themselves narrowly on the Sunni community there are limits to their size and prospects. They cannot 'win' although they can cause a lot of death and destruction. If other countries succumb, it will only be because the militants have found ways of exploiting social and political divisions that are already well established. These methods are never sufficient to kick-start campaigns: they only work to move them into more confrontational stages.

To what extent can it be said that there has been a transformation of strategic affairs? The international system has certainly been transformed. The most important, and welcome, change has been the decline in inter-state wars and of great power confrontation in general. This is part of a broader, and also positive, drift downwards in the incidence and impact of wars of all types. The Canadian Human Security Centre reports that the world is tangibly becoming more peaceful: the number of armed conflicts has declined by more than 40% since 1992. There are now fewer international crises and military coups than ever before. Wars are less deadly and less money is spent on arms. Only international terrorism is increasing.[29] Western armed forces face a narrowing of the range of contingencies for which their use might be contemplated. They cannot be sure which contingencies will prompt a decision by their governments to intervene, but they can assume that if they are asked to engage this will be in a conflict that is already underway and tending towards irregular warfare.

Regular warfare cannot be ruled out and, arguably, remains unlikely only because of the deterrent effect of continuing to make substantial provision for it. Some recent conflicts have involved operations that resemble past battles in pitting conventionally organised forces against each other. Preparing for such battles has long been the main business of the military. Thinking about regular warfare offers strategists a sort of comfort zone, where conflict will be governed by familiar principles and sets understood requirements for the development of capabilities, doctrine and training. Irregular warfare, by contrast, is unfamiliar and perplexing, lacking obvious boundaries. The range of forms it can take is disorienting, taking in guerrilla struggle, warlord rivalries and gangsterism, inter-communal violence and mass-casualty terrorism. The standards of victory can be equally confusing, especially when (as is usually the case) no culminating point is reached. These conflicts often either peter out or are marginalised by political developments, with the militants neither seizing power nor surrendering. Unlike regular warfare, irregular conflicts are unlikely to turn on having the most advanced technology or the imposition of overwhelming force. The military role may be quite limited, with key tasks in the hands of intelligence agencies and the police, and with even political leaders and intellectuals who frame and describe the core issues at the heart of the struggle. Whoever takes the lead, success will depend on how a particular irregular war's purpose, course and conduct is viewed by public opinion at home as well as within the theatre of operations. Success in such warfare depends on an understanding of behaviour and attitudes, and so science and engineering may provide fewer clues about its future than sociological and anthropological assessments of questions of identity and social cohesion.

As always, some history might also be helpful. Though irregular war requires a shift in focus, the issues raised are hardly novel. Those who served in the anti-colonial wars of the twentieth century would recognise many of the dilemmas faced by their contemporary counterparts as they try to think of ways to win over sullen populations by offering current security and hope for the future, acquiring reliable intelligence, setting traps while avoiding obvious ambushes, flushing out militants and turning some into informers, building up credible local leadership while catching or discrediting those of the enemy, and dividing and ruling through judicious use of amnesties and political initiatives. They might be shocked by the media gaze that ensures that these efforts are watched and evaluated constantly and globally, so that every mistake and false move is broadcast immediately, and constant difficulty is experienced in distinguishing minor tactical success from major strategic advances. But they might also conclude that this reinforces the lessons of past conflicts, that acquiring or retaining the trust and confidence of populations requires sensitivity to their concerns and treating them with respect. This can then be the basis of a compelling strategic narrative. This is not simply a matter of presentational skills, to be handed over to a public affairs unit. In this regard, developing a narrative is not a strategy in itself. If a convincing narrative can be constructed, that will normally be because the underlying strategy is sound and because it speaks to established belief systems, which in the case of the US and its allies, must mean to liberal values.

NOTES

Introduction

[1] John Keegan, *A History of Warfare* (New York: Knopf, 1993); Martin van Creveld, *The Transformation of War* (New York: Free Press, 1991); General Sir Rupert Smith, *The Utility Of Force: The Art of War in the Modern World* (London: Allen Lane, 2005).

[2] Norman Angell, *The Great Illusion* (London: William Heinemann, 1914); Walter Millis, *An End to Arms* (New York: Atheneum Press, 1964). See also van Creveld (fn 1).

[3] On the argument that suicide bombing can be understood in strategic terms see Robert A. Pape, *Dying to Win: The Strategic Logic of Suicide Terrorism* (New York: Random House, 2005).

[4] Lawrence Freedman, *Adelphi Paper 318. The Revolution in Strategic Affairs.* (Oxford: Oxford University Press, 1998).

Chapter One

[1] Actually, if you want to knock a body off balance the worst place to aim for is the centre of gravity.

[2] US Department of Defense, *Field Manual 100-5: Operations* (Washington DC: Department of the Army, 1982), vol. 2-1.

[3] Anthony H. Cordesman and Abraham R. Wagner, *The Lessons of Modern War, Vol. IV: The Gulf War* (Boulder, CO: Westview, 1996).

[4] Barry D. Watts, 'Effects and Effectiveness', in Eliot A. Cohen, ed., *Gulf War Air Power Survey, Vol. 2: Operations and Effects and Effectiveness* (Washington DC: GPO, 1993), p. 363.

[5] Important articles in defining the RMA were Andrew F. Krepinevich, 'Cavalry to Computer: The Pattern of Military Revolutions', *The National Interest*, no. 37, Fall 1994; William A. Owens, 'The Emerging System of Systems', *US Naval Institute Proceedings*, May 1995, pp. 36–39; and Eliot A. Cohen, 'A Revolution in Warfare', *Foreign Affairs*, vol. 75, no. 2, March/April 1996. For an analysis of the various theories see Colin S. Gray, *Strategy for Chaos: Revolutions in Military Affairs and The Evidence of History* (London: Frank Cass, 2002).

[6] Robert H. Scales, *Yellow Smoke: The Future of Land Warfare for America's Military* (Lanham, MD: Rowman & Littlefield, 2003).

[7] US Department of Defense, *Quadrennial Defense Review Report* (Washington DC: Department of Defense, February 2006). The full text is available to download from: http://www.dod.gov/qdr/report/Report20060203.pdf.

[8] Even compared with the *National Defense Strategy* document of March 2005, which

set its foundations, there is a sharper
focus on dealing with the new threats and
less emphasis on conventional military
operations. US Department of Defense,
National Defense Strategy (Washington
DC: Department of Defense, March
2005). The full text is available to down-
load from: http://www.defenselink.
mil/news/Mar2005/d20050318nds1.pdf.
For a critique of the QDR see Michèle
A. Flournoy, 'Did the Pentagon Get the
Quadrennial Defense Review Right?',
The Washington Quarterly, vol. 29, no. 2,
Spring 2006, pp. 67–84.

9   The White House, *The National Security
Strategy of the United States of America*
(Washington DC: The White House,
September 2002). The full text is available
to download from: http://www.white-
house.gov/nsc/nss.pdf.

10 An influential book in this regard was
Alvin Toffler and Heidi Toffler, *War and
Anti-War: Survival at the Dawn of the 21st
Century* (New York: Little, Brown & Co.,
1993).

11 Steven Metz, *Armed Conflict in the 21st
Century: the Information Revolution
and Post-Modern Warfare* (Carlisle, PA:
Strategic Studies Institute, 2000).

12 'Information technology might provide
a politically usable way to damage an
enemy's national or commercial infrastructure badly enough to attain victory
without having to first defeat fielded military forces'. Ibid.

13 John Arquilla and David Ronfeldt, 'The
Advent of Netwar: Analytic Background',
Studies in Conflict and Terrorism, vol. 22,
no. 3, July–September 1999.

14 Jerrold M. Post, Keven G. Ruby and Eric D.
Shaw, 'From Car Bombs to Logic Bombs:
The Growing Threat from Information
Terrorism', *Terrorism and Political Violence*,
vol. 12, no. 2, Summer 2000, pp. 102–3.

15 US Joint Chiefs of Staff, *Joint Publication 3-
13: Joint Doctrine for Information Operations*
(Washington DC: GPO, October 1998), p.
GL-7.

16 William M. Arkin, 'Spiraling ahead: With
the loss of its greatest champion, what's to

become of transformation?', *Armed Forces
Journal*, February 2006. For a full statement
of Van Riper's views see 'Information
Superiority': Statement before the
Procurement Subcommittee and Research
and Development Subcommittee of the
House National Security Committee in
Congress on 20 March 1998: http://www.
comw.org/rma/fulltext/infosup.html.

17 Timothy L. Thomas, 'Kosovo and the
Current Myth of Information Superiority',
Parameters, vol. 30, no. 1, Spring 2000, pp.
13–29.

18 'At the structural level, network-centric
warfare requires an operational architec-
ture with three critical elements: sensor
grids and transaction (or engagement)
grids hosted by a high-quality information backplane. They are supported by
value-adding command-and-control
processes, many of which must be auto-
mated to get required speed.' Cebrowski
and Garstka, 'Network-Centric Warfare:
Its Origin and Future', *US Naval Institute
Proceedings*, January 1998.

19 As developed by John Boyd. See Robert
Coram, *Boyd: The Fighter Pilot Who
Changed the Art of War* (New York: Little,
Brown & Co., 2002).

20 US Department of Defense Report
to Congress, *Network Centric Warfare*
(Washington DC: Department of Defense,
July 2001), p. iv.

21 Major Norman Emery, US Army, Major
Jason Werchan, US Air Force and Major
Donald G. Mowles, US Air Force, 'Fighting
Terrorism and Insurgency: Shaping
the Information Environment', *Military
Review*, January–February 2005, pp. 32–38.

22 Arquilla and Ronfeldt, eds, *Networks and
Netwars: The Future of Terror, Crime, and
Militancy* (Santa Monica, CA: RAND,
2001). The full text is available at: www.
rand.org/publications/MR/MR1382/.
For a summary of their arguments,
see Ronfeldt and Arquilla 'Networks,
Netwars, and the Fight for the Future',
First Monday, vol. 6, no. 10, October 2001:
http://firstmonday.org/issues/issue6_10/
ronfeldt/index.html.

[23] William S. Lind, Colonel Keith Nightengale, Captain John F. Schmitt, Colonel Joseph W. Sutton and Lieutenant Colonel Gary I. Wilson, 'The Changing Face of War: Into the Fourth Generation', *Marine Corps Gazette*, October 1989, pp. 22–26; Lind, 'Understanding Fourth Generation War', *Military Review*, September–October 2004, pp. 12–16. This reports the findings of a study group which he convened at his house.

[24] Hammes, 'War Evolves into the Fourth Generation', *Contemporary Security Policy*, vol. 26, no. 2, August 2005. This issue contains a number of critiques of the idea of fourth-generation warfare, including one by the author. For a full account of Hammes's ideas see *The Sling And the Stone: On War in the 21st Century* (St Paul, MN: Zenith Press, 2004).

[25] Lind presents anything corrosive of the cultural foundations of a society as part of such a war. Cultural damage appeared as the product of deliberate and hostile moves by enemies, aided and abetted by naïve and wrong-thinking elements at home, rather than of broader and more diffuse social trends or economic imperatives. See Bill Berkowitz, 'A mighty Lind', September 2003. http://www.workingfor-change.com/article.cfm?ItemID=15659.

[26] Scales, 'Culture-Centric Warfare', *US Naval Institute Proceedings*, October 2004.

[27] Arquilla and Ronfeldt (eds), *Networks and Netwars*.

[28] See for example Robert Fulford, *The Triumph of Narrative: Storytelling in the Age of Mass Culture* (Toronto: Anansi, 1999); Jay Rosen, 'PressThink Basics: The Master Narrative in Journalism', September 2003. http://journalism.nyu.edu/pubzone/weblogs/pressthink/2003/09/08/basics_master.html.

[29] Cohen, *Supreme Command: Soldiers, Statesmen, and Leadership in Wartime* (New York: The Free Press, 2002).

[30] Freedman, 'War in Iraq: Selling the Threat', *Survival*, vol. 46, no. 2, Summer 2004, pp. 7–50.

[31] Jay Rosen, 'Theoretical Foundations: Public Journalism as a Democratic Art', July 2002, http://www.imdp.org/artman/publish/printer_23.shtml.

[32] William D. Caseebeer and James A. Russell, 'Storytelling and Terrorism: Towards a Comprehensive "Counter-Narrative Strategy"', *Strategic Insights*, vol. IV, no. 3, March 2005.

Chapter Two

[1] A recent article claims that globalisation had some responsibility for the First World War. See David M. Rowe, 'The Tragedy of Liberalism: How Globalization Caused the First World War', *Security Studies*, vol. 14, no. 3, Spring 2005, pp. 407–447.

[2] The leaked draft of the Department of Defense's *Defense Planning Guidance for the Fiscal Years 1994–1999* of 18 February 1992 was published in the *New York Times* on 8 March 1992.

[3] John J. Mearsheimer, 'Back to the Future: Instability in Europe After the Cold War', *International Security*, Vol. 15, No. 1, Summer 1990, pp. 5–56. See also Mearsheimer, *The Tragedy of Great Power Politics* (New York: W.W. Norton & Company, 2001).

[4] For a sceptical view see Gerald Segal, 'Does China Matter?', *Foreign Affairs*, vol. 78, no. 5, September/October 1999. Segal's views were assessed in Barry Buzan and Rosemary Foot, eds, *Does China Matter? A Reassessment* (Abingdon: Routledge, 2004). For a more recent assessment of Chinese thinking see Avery Goldstein, *Rising to the Challenge: China's Grand Strategy and International Security* (Palo Alto, CA: Stanford University Press, 2005).

[5] Stephen M. Walt, *Taming American Power: The Global Response to US Primacy* (New York: W.W. Norton, 2005).

6 Freedman, 'The Gulf war and the new world order', *Survival* , vol. 33, no. 3, May/June 1991.

7 Freedman, 'The age of liberal wars', *Review of International Studies*, forthcoming 2006.

8 Michael Howard, *War and the Liberal Conscience: The George Trevelyan Lectures in the University of Cambridge, 1977* (London: Maurice Temple Smith, 1978), pp. 134–5.

9 Joseph S. Nye, *Soft Power: The Means to Success in World Politics* (New York: PublicAffairs, 2004).

10 The constructivist literature in international relations has shown more interest in ideas about the meaning of great power and the nature of the international system, and their influence on foreign policy, than the role of ideologies. Jeffrey W. Legro's, *Rethinking the World: Great Power Strategies and International Order* (Ithaca, NY: Cornell University Press, 2005) is a good example of this although it deals with both the Soviet Union and China.

11 For an analysis of the problem of self-defence in similar terms see James Gow, *Defending the West* (Cambridge: Polity Press, 2005).

12 Report of the International Commission on Intervention and State Sovereignty, *The Responsibility To Protect* (Ottawa: International Development Research Centre, December 2001). The full text is available to download from: http://www.iciss.ca/pdf/Commission-Report.pdf.

13 Objectives could be set for military intervention as a result of exaggerated expectations for non-military forms of coercion. The European Union and the UN made demands on the former Yugoslavia which could not be enforced via trade embargoes and diplomatic isolation. Either they had to abandon their initial position (with a consequent loss of authority) or consider escalation. The prudent military planner, therefore, would start work as soon as an explicit international commitment to a particular outcome for a particular conflict had been made, even though the possibility of military enforcement was being excluded at the time.

14 This distinction is developed further in Freedman, *Adelphi Paper 318. The Revolution in Strategic Affairs.*

15 Weinberger, *Fighting for Peace: Seven Critical Years in the Pentagon* (New York: Warner Books, 1990), pp. 453–4. See Kenneth Campbell, 'Once Burned, Twice Cautious: Explaining the Weinberger–Powell Doctrine', *Armed Forces and Society*, vol. 24, no. 3, Spring 1998. It has been noted that application of the Weinberger tests in 1965 would probably have permitted entry into the Vietnam War.

16 White Paper presented to the UK parliament by the Secretary of State for Defence, *Strategic Defence Review*, July 1998: http://www.mod.uk/issues/sdr/wp_contents.htm.

17 'Doctrine of the International Community', speech by Tony Blair to the Economic Club, Chicago, 24 April 1999: http://www.number-10.gov.uk/output/Page1297.asp.

Chapter Three

1 See James Turner Johnson, *Morality and Contemporary Warfare* (New Haven, CT: Yale University Press, 1999).

2 The various views on the future role of nuclear weapons can be found in the contributions to John Baylis and Robert O'Neill, eds, *Alternative Nuclear Futures : The Role of Nuclear Weapons in the Post-Cold War World* (Oxford: Oxford University Press, 1999).

3 President Clinton was apparently persuaded of the potential risks of biotechnological warfare by the novel *The Cobra Event* by Richard Preston, in which a terrorist releases an engineered virus in New York, causing auto-cannibalism.

4 Andrew Mack, 'Why Big Nations Lose Small Wars: The Politics of Asymmetric Conflict', *World Politics*, vol. 27, no. 2, January 1975, pp. 175–200.

5 'Asymmetric engagements are battles between dissimilar forces'. US Joint Chiefs of Staff, *Joint Publication 1: Joint Warfare of the Armed Forces of the United States* (Washington DC: GPO, January 1995), p. iv.

6 Cited in John T. Correll, 'Casualties', *Air Force Magazine*, June 2003, p. 49.

7 Secretary of Defense William S. Cohen, *Report of the Quadrennial Defense Review* (Washington DC: Department of Defense, May 1997), Section II.

8 US Joint Chiefs of Staff, *Joint Vision 2020* (Washington DC: GPO, 2000), p. 5. The full text is available to download from: http://www.dtic.mil/jointvision/jvpub2.htm. The following paragraph draws heavily on Metz and Douglas V. Johnson, *Asymmetry and U.S. Military Strategy: Definition, Background, and Strategic Concepts* (Carlisle, PA: Strategic Studies Institute, 2001).

9 US Joint Chiefs of Staff, *Joint Strategy Review 1999* (Washington DC: GPO, 1999), p. 2.

10 US Joint Chiefs of Staff, *Joint Vision 2010* (Washington DC: GPO, 2000). The full text is available to download from: http://www.dtic.mil/jv2010/jv2010.pdf.

11 *Report of the Quadrennial Defense Review* (Washington DC: Department of Defense, September 2001), p. 21, http://www.defenselink.mil/pubs/qdr2001.pdf. A former Secretary of Defense, William J. Perry, also gave the impression that the most important policy response to the terrorist attacks would be in the area of missile defence, in 'Preparing for the Next Attack', *Foreign Affairs*, vol. 80, no. 6, November/December 2001, pp. 31–45.

12 The United States Commission on National Security/21st Century, *New World Coming: American Security in the 21st Century* (Washington DC: Department of Defense, 1999), p. 48. For a similar emphasis see also National Commission on Terrorism, *Countering the Changing Threat of International Terrorism: Pursuant to Public Law 277, 105th Congress* (Washington DC: US Congress, 2000). This also focused on a state-sponsored, mass casualty, catastrophic attack and implied that US policy might be too heavily focused on Osama bin Laden. Similarly, a major study by the Center for Strategic and International Studies (CSIS), with many thoughtful recommendations to improve homeland defence, made national missile defence the priority issue, and focused on chemical, biological, nuclear and radiological weapons and cyber-terrorism. Frank Cilluffo et al., *Defending America in the 21st Century: New Challenges, New Organizations, and New Policies: Executive Summary of Four CSIS Working Group Reports on Homeland Defense* (Washington DC: CSIS, 2000).

13 Interview by Andrew Herson, *Policy Review*, Summer 1993, p. 145, cited in Richard Eichenberg, 'Victory Has Many Friends: U.S. Public Opinion and the Use of Military Force, 1981–2005', *International Security*, vol. 30, no. 1, Summer 2005, pp. 140–77.

14 Richard Holbrooke, *To End a War* (New York: Random House, 1999).

15 Edward N. Luttwak, 'Toward Post-Heroic Warfare', *Foreign Affairs*, vol. 74, no. 3, May/June 1995, pp. 109–22.

16 John Mueller, *War, Presidents and Public Opinion* (New York: Wiley, 1973).

17 Eichenberg, 'Victory Has Many Friends'. See also James Burk, 'Public Support for Peacekeeping in Lebanon and Somalia: Assessing the Casualties Hypothesis', *Political Science Quarterly*, vol. 114, no. 1, Spring 1999, pp. 53–78; Eric V. Larson, *Casualties and Consensus: The Historical Role of Casualties in Domestic Support for U.S. Military Operations* (Santa Monica, CA: RAND, 1996); Steven Kull and Clay Ramsay, 'The Myth of the Reactive Public: American Public Attitudes on Military Fatalities in the Post-Cold War Period', in Philip Everts and Pierangelo Isernia, eds, *Public Opinion and the International Use of Force* (London: Routledge, 2001), pp. 205–28. A recent literature review concludes 'there is no convincing evidence that casualty aversion has become the dominant factor in determining the use or non-use of force by democracies'. Hugh Smith, 'What Costs will Democracies Bear? A Review of Popular Theories of Casualty Aversion', *Armed Forces & Society*, vol. 31, no. 4, Summer 2005, p. 508.

18 In other contingencies involving Taiwan and Iraq the acceptable levels were much higher but the ordering of tolerance, with the public most relaxed, remained the same. The results were reported by Peter D. Feaver and Christopher Gelpi, *Choosing Your Battles: American Civil–Military Relations and the Use of Force* (Princeton, NJ: Princeton University Press, 2003). For a discussion of all relevant findings see Charles Hyde, 'Casualty Aversion: Implications for Policy Makers and Senior Military Officers', *Aerospace Power Journal*, vol. 14, no. 2, Summer 2000, pp. 17–27.

19 Cited in Andrew Erdmann, 'The U.S. Presumption of Quick, Costless Wars', *Orbis*, vol. 43, no. 3, Summer 1999, pp. 363–81.

20 Jeffrey Record, 'Force-Protection Fetishism: Sources, Consequences, and (?) Solutions', *Aerospace Power Journal*, vol. 14, no. 2, Summer 2000, p. 5.

21 Prepared joint statement on the Kosovo After Action Review presented by Secretary of Defense William S. Cohen and General Henry H. Shelton, Chairman of the Joint Chiefs of Staff, before the Senate Armed Services Committee, October 14, 1999, http://www.defenselink.mil/news/Oct1999/b10141999_bt478-99.html.

22 Interview with CNN's Peter Arnett, 11 May 1997.

23 Report of the National Defense Panel, *Transforming Defense: National Security in the 21st Century* (Washington DC: Department of Defense, December 1997), p. 1. The report is available to download from: http://www.dtic.mil/ndp/FullDoc2.pdf. Douglas A. MacGregor, *Breaking the Phalanx: A New Design for Landpower in the 21st Century* (Westport, CT: Praeger, 1997).

24 Colin Powell and Joseph Persico, *My American Journey: An Autobiography* (New York: Random House, 1995). See also Charles Stevenson, 'The Evolving Clinton Doctrine on the Use of Force', *Armed Forces and Society*, vol. 22, no. 4, Summer 1996, pp. 511–35.

25 Colin Powell, 'U.S. Forces: Challenges Ahead', vol. 71, no. 5, *Foreign Affairs*, Winter 1992/93, pp. 32–45.

26 The distinction was developed under Powell's guidance in the US Department of Defense, *Joint Pub 3-0: Doctrine for Joint Operations* (Washington DC: Joint Chiefs of Staff, 1993). See Stevenson, 'The Evolving Clinton Doctrine', p. 517.

27 Andrew J. Bacevich, *The New American Militarism: How Americans are Seduced by War* (New York: Oxford University Press, 2005).

28 Cohen, 'Constraints on America's Conduct of Small Wars', *International Security*, vol. 9, no. 2, Fall 1984, pp. 151–81.

29 Cited in Larry Cable, 'Reinventing the Round Wheel: Insurgency, Counter-Insurgency, and Peacekeeping Post Cold War', *Small Wars and Insurgencies*, vol. 4, no. 2, Autumn 1993, pp. 228–62.

30 Clark, *Waging Modern War: Bosnia, Kosovo and the Future of Conflict* (New York: PublicAffairs, 2001).

31 Joint Chiefs of Staff, *Joint Vision 2010*, p. 1.

32 Douglas Lovelace, Jr, *The Evolution of Military Affairs: Shaping the Future U.S. Armed Forces* (Carlisle, PA: Strategic Studies Institute, 1997).

33 Jennifer M. Taw and Alan Vick, 'From Sideshow to Center Stage: The Role of the Army and Air Force in Military Operations Other Than War', in Zalmay M. Khalilzad and David A. Ochmanek, eds, *Strategy and Defense Planning for the 21st Century* (Santa Monica, CA: RAND & US Air Force, 1997), pp. 208–209.

34 Condoleezza Rice, 'Campaign 2000: Promoting the National Interest', *Foreign Affairs*, vol. 79, no. 1, January/February 2000, p. 53.

Chapter Four

1 See above, p. 11. Colonel J. Warden, USAF, *The Air Campaign: Planning for Combat* (Washington DC: NDU, 1988).

2 *Report of the Panel on United Nations Peace Operations* (Brahimi Report), United Nations, August 2000, http://www.un.org/peace/reports/peace_operations/.

3 Robert C. Owen, 'The Balkans Air Campaign Study: Part Two', *Airpower Journal*, vol. 11, no. 3, Fall 1997, pp. 6–26.

4 John A. Tirpak, 'Deliberate Force' *Air Force Magazine*, vol. 80, no. 10, October 1997, pp. 36–43.

5 See Holbrooke, *To End a War*.

6 John Keegan, 'So the Bomber Got Through After All', *Daily Telegraph*, 4 June 1999. For a sceptical view see E.H. Tilford, 'Operation Allied Force and the Role of Air Power', *Parameters*, vol. 29, no.4, Winter 1999–2000, pp.6–26. For assessments of the war, see Tim Judah, *Kosovo: War and Revenge* (New Haven, CT: Yale University Press, 2000); and Albrecht Schnabel and Ramesh Thakur, eds, *Kosovo and the Challenge of Humanitarian Intervention: Selective Indignation, Collective Action, and International Citizenship* (Tokyo: United Nations University Press, 2000). On the issue of humanitarian intervention, see Adam Roberts, 'NATO's "Humanitarian War" over Kosovo', *Survival*, vol. 4l, no. 3, Autumn 1999, pp. 102–23.

7 Edward Cody, 'Taliban's Hide-and-Wait Tactics Tied to U.S. Aversion to Casualties', *International Herald Tribune*, 22 October 2001.

8 Remarks by the President at the Citadel, Charleston, South Carolina, 11 December 2001.

9 Interview broadcast on CBS 'Face the Nation', 18 November 2001. A transcript is available at http://www.defenselink.mil/transcripts/2001/t11182001_t1118wol.html.

10 George Packer, *The Assassin's Gate: America in Iraq* (New York: Farrar, Straus and Giroux, 2005).

11 Hearings, *Department Of Defense Budget Priorities For Fiscal Year 2004*, Committee on the Budget One Hundred Eighth Congress: First Session, 27 February 2003.

12 'American Army Tactics in Iraq', *The Economist*, 29 December 2004.

Chapter Five

1. Gladys Ganley, 'Power to the People via Personal Electronic Media', *The Washington Quarterly*, vol. 14, no. 2, Spring 1991, pp. 5–26.

2. *Internet Filtering in China in 2004–2005: A Country Study*, http://www.opennetinitia-tive.net/studies/china/.

3. Steve Coll and Susan B. Glasser, 'Terrorists Turn to the Web as Base of Operations', *Washington Post*, 7 August 2005. See also Timothy L. Thomas, 'Al Qaeda and the Internet: The Danger of "Cyberplanning"', *Parameters*, Spring 2003, pp. 112–23.

4. Jean Seaton, 'Why Do We Think The Serbs Do It? The New "Ethnic" Wars and the Media', *Political Quarterly*, vol. 70, no. 3, July–September 1999, p. 261.

5. Matt Stoller, 'The Narrative as Battlefield', 14 December 2003, http://www.bopnews.com/archives/000084.html.

6. The text of the letter is available in English from the Office of the Director of National Intelligence: http://www.dni.gov/release_letter_101105.html.

7. James Gow and James Tilsey, 'The Strategic Imperative for Media Management' in James Gow, Richard Paterson and Alison Preston, eds, *Bosnia by Television* (London: British Film Institute, 1996), p. 107.

8. Gow and Tilsey, Ibid., pp. 109–10. For an analysis of the same episode, as part of a general critique on the loss of journalistic objectivity during the conflict see John Burns, 'The Media as Impartial Observers or Protagonists' in *Bosnia by Television*, pp. 96–7. For those in charge of the international organisations operating on the ground, including the United Nations Protection Force, this eroded sympathy for people who, they felt, were constantly playing with the truth in order to influence world opinion. It encouraged the perception that 'they are all as bad each other' and mutual irritation as local UN commanders were obliged to challenge the accounts of their local interlocutors. This is reflected in the memoir of General Sir Michael Rose, *Fighting for Peace: Bosnia, 1994* (London: The Harvill Press, 1998). For a critique see Michael Williams, 'Perceptions of the war in Bosnia', *International Affairs*, vol. 75, no. 2, April 1999, pp. 377–382.

9. In Philip Seib, *Headline Diplomacy: How News Coverage Affects Foreign Policy* (Boulder, CO: Praeger, 1997), p. 135.

10. Walter Goodman, cited in Miles Hudson and John Stanier, *War and the Media*, revised edn (Stroud: Sutton Publishing, 1999), p. 256.

11. *The Times*, 18 August 1992, cited in Martin Bell, *In Harm's Way* (London: Hamish Hamilton, 1995), p. 137.

12. Piers Robinson, 'The CNN effect: can the news media drive foreign policy?, *Review of International Studies*, vol. 25, no. 2, April 1999, pp. 301–09. The original CNN effect, it might be noted, referred to the ubiquity of the channel (so that all sides were using the same information source) as much as to the particulars of its effects. The term itself originated during the Gulf War and was naturally promoted by CNN's owner, Ted Turner. See Thomas B. Allen, F. Clifton Berry and Norman Polmar, *CNN: War in the Gulf* (Atlanta, GA: Turner Broadcasting, 1991).

13. The origins go back to a letter from John Adams to Thomas Jefferson of 19 April 1817. The American Revolution, he observed, 'was effected before the war commenced. The Revolution was in the minds and hearts of the people; a change in their religious sentiments, of their duties and obligations...This radical change in the principles, opinions, sentiments, and affections of the people was the real American Revolution'.

14. Kaplan, *Imperial Grunts: The American Military on the Ground*, (New York: Random House, 2005).

15. Cited Aylwin-Foster, 'Changing the Army for Counterinsurgency Operations', *Military Review*, November–December 2005, p. 5.

16 Montgonery McFate, 'The Military Utility of Understanding Adversary Culture', *Joint Forces Quarterly*, no. 38, July 2005, p. 44.

17 Aylwin-Foster, 'Changing the Army for Counterinsurgency Operations', p. 4.

18 Thomas E. Ricks, 'Lessons Learned in Iraq Show Up in Army Classes: Culture Shifts to Counterinsurgency', *Washington Post*, 21 January 2006.

19 Scales, *Culture-Centric Warfare*. It is instructive to compare these proposals with remarkably similar ideas that were propounded in the late 1950s as the Americans were encouraged to pay more attention to the third world. See in particular William J. Lederer and Eugene Burdick, *The Ugly American* (New York: Fawcett House, 1958).

20 Daniel Byman, *Going To War With The Allies You Have: Allies, Counterinsurgency, And The War On Terrorism* (Carlisle, PA: Strategic Studies Institute, November 2005).

21 Pew Global Attitudes Project, 'U.S. Image Up Slightly, But Still Negative: American Character Gets Mixed Reviews', 23 June 2005: http://pewglobal.org/reports/display.php?PageID=800.

22 The term 'public diplomacy' was first used in 1965 by Edmund Gullion, a career foreign service diplomat and subsequently dean of the Fletcher School of Law and Diplomacy at Tufts University, in connection with the establishment at the Fletcher School of the Edward R. Murrow Center for Public Diplomacy. Charles Wolf, Jr and Brian Rosen, 'Public Diplomacy: Lessons from King and Mandela', *Policy Review*, no. 33, October/November 2005.

23 Byman, 'Al-Qaeda as an Adversary: Do we understand our enemy?', *World Politics*, vol. 56, no. 1, October 2003, pp. 162–3.

24 Rumsfeld, 'War of the Words', *Wall Street Journal*, 18 July 2005. The Pentagon website is www.defenselink.mil.

25 Rumsfeld, 'New Realities in the Media Age', speech delivered at the Council on Foreign Relations, New York, 17 February 2006: http://www.cfr.org/publication/9900/. A few days later his British counterpart, Dr John Reid, made similar points in a speech to the War Studies Department at King's College London. 'One observer, with one videophone, or today even one mobile phone, standing in one square metre of a vast and hugely complex theatre of operations can convey an oversimplified and sometimes misleading picture with an impact that is incalculable.' http://www.mod.uk/DefenceInternet/DefenceNews/DefencePolicyAndBusiness/WeMustBeslowerToCondemnQuickerToUnderstandTheForcesJohnReid.htm.

26 Safire, 'Insurgent irresponsiveness', *International Herald Tribune*, 16 January 2006. In developing his theme of how in wartime words are weapons, Safire notes how the Israelis lost the battle in attempting to call the land west of the Jordan River by the biblical Judea and Samaria, or even 'administered territories'.

27 Scott Shane, 'Bush's Iraq speech echoes a new voice', *International Herald Tribune*, 4 December 2005.

28 Jeff Gerth, 'Military's Information War Is Vast and Often Secretive', *New York Times*, 12 December 2005.

29 Human Security Centre, *Human Security Report 2005: War and Peace in the 21st Century* (New York: Oxford University Press, 2006). The full report can be downloaded from: http://www.humansecurityreport.info/.

RECENT **ADELPHI PAPERS** INCLUDE:

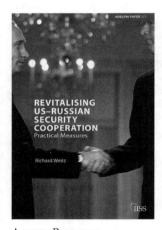

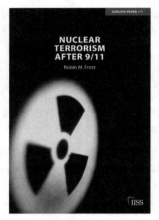

ADELPHI PAPER 377
**Revitalising US–Russian
Security Cooperation:**
Practical Measures

Richard Weitz

ISBN 0-415-39864-9

ADELPHI PAPER 378
Nuclear Terrorism After 9/11
Robin M. Frost

ISBN 0-415-39992-0